# TURKISH COOKERY

İnci Kut

**NET**®

**TURİSTİK YAYINLAR**
**SANAYİ VE TİCARET A.Ş.**

Published and distributed by:

**NET TURİSTİK YAYINLAR A.Ş.**

**Şifa Hamamı Sok. No. 18/2, 34400 Sultanahmet-İstanbul/Turkey**
**Tel: (90-212) 516 32 28 - 516 82 61 Fax: (90-212) 516 84 68**

**236. Sokak No.96/B Funda Apt., 35360 Hatay/İzmir/Turkey**
**Tel:(90-232) 228 78 51 - 250 69 22 Fax: (90-232) 250 22 73**

**Kışla Mah., 54. Sok., İlteray Apt., No.11/A-B, 07040 Antalya/Turkey**
**Tel: (90-242) 248 93 67 - 243 14 97 Fax: (90-242) 248 93 68**

**Eski Kayseri Cad., Dirikoçlar Apt. No.45, 50200 Nevşehir/Turkey**
**Tel: (90-384) 213 30 89 - 213 46 20 Fax: (90-384) 213 40 36**

Text: **İnci Kut**
Photographs: **Haluk Konyalı G.S.A.**
Layout: **Not Ajans**
Typesetting: **AS&64 Ltd. Şti.**
Colour separation: **Mas Matbaacılık A.Ş.**
Printed in Turkey by: **Asır Matbaacılık A.Ş.**

**ISBN 975-479-100-7**

# CONTENTS

# CONTENTS

# TURKISH FOOD

The culinary art in Turkey is made of a great variety of delicious dishes which are a mixture of various delicacies inherited from different regions of the vast Ottoman Empire, while unfortunately many of them have long been forgotten through the centures.
Amont different parts of the Turkish Cookery, the most notable are: hors d'oeuvres (meze); pastries (börek) filled with meat, cheese, vegetables or any other filling depending on the imagination; stuffed vegetables and vine leaves (dolma) of two different kinds with meat or rice; broiled or roasted meat dishes (kebab and köfte); different kinds of rice dishes (pilâv); and finally vegetables cooked in olive oil (zeytinyağlı). This last one is particularly notable: a certain vegetable is cooked with onions and tomatoes in abundant olive oil and garnished with salt, sugar and sometimes garlic, and served cold. Egg-plant in olive oil, the famous "imambayıldı" is particularly worth mentioning. It means "the imam fainted", but the legend does not clarify whether the imam fainted because of the tastiness of the dish, or because of the great amount of olive oil used in it!
After such a great variety of delicious dishes, the desserts also take a great part. In Turkey, apart from the European type pastry-shops, there are special and traditional milk pudding and sweet pastry shops.
A rich Turkish table is always finished off with the famous Turkish coffee; which is well toasted and finely ground coffee simmered with or without sugar in a special long-handled pot called "cezve".
The most popular and typical dishes among the Turkish cookery have been selected for this book.
Good appetite!

# DETAILS ABOUT SOME INGREDIENTS

**Nuts and raisins:** In Turkey there is a large variety of nuts which are used for decorating desserts. However, a special one, pine nuts, is also indispensable for rice fillings and some other rice dishes, together with dried black currants. Sultanas are used only for desserts.

**Olive oil:** It is largely used in Turkish cookery, not only in salad dressings but for a great variety of vegetable dishes which are cooked with olive oil and served cool.

**Onion and garlic:** Onions are indispensable for the preparation of Turkish food and salads. Garlic is also a very important ingredient, especially to flavour the yoghurt which is frequently served with many meat and vegetable dishes.

**Turkish white cheese:** It is an uncooked cheese made from sheep milk, largely used as pastry filling, apart from being served for breakfast.

**"Yufka" (philo dough):** These are ready made, very thin, big and round sheets of dough used for various kinds of pastries (börek), baked of fried. If you have to prepare the dough yourself for some of the Turkish recipes, you will need an 80 cm. long rolling pin as thin as a finger (oklava). This is the only way to roll out paper thin sheets of dough for the famous flaky pastries.

**Minced meat:** It is largely used in Turkish cookery, either prepared as various kinds of meatballs (köfte) or sauté with onions to garnish various vegetable dishes, or mixed with other ingredients to be used as a filling for pastries and stuffed vegetables. It is sometimes a mixture of beef and mutton and always minced twice. In Turkey, the butcher knows what kind of minced meat should be for which dish.

## MEASUREMENTS

| | Milk | Melted butter and oil | Rice | Wheat, dry beans, lentils | Semolina, castor sugar | Flour | Sugar | Grated cheese | Crushed almonds and walnuts | Bread crumbs |
|---|---|---|---|---|---|---|---|---|---|---|
| 1 glass of 25 cl. of water, contains | 25 cl. | 220 gr. | 230 gr. | 200 gr. | 180 gr. | 160 gr. | 240 gr. | 100 gr. | 100 gr. | 100 gr. |
| 1 tea cup of 15 cl. of water, contains | 15 cl. | 130 gr. | 130 gr. | 120 gr. | 110 gr. | 100 gr. | 140 gr. | 50 gr. | 50 gr. | 50 gr. |

1 glass of 25 cl. = 1 U.S. cup = 5/6 British breakfast cup
1 cup of 15 cl. = 3/5 U.S. cup = 1/2 British breakfast cup
1 litre (liquid) = 3.8 quarts
1 ounce = 28,3 gr.

1 pound = 453,5 gr.
1 U.S. liquid pint = 0,473 lt.
1 English pint = 0,568 lt.

Different kinds of soups can be served as entrée at a Turkish table.

The most well known soup among all is the tripe soup, which is especialy good late at night, at the end of a long friedly gathering over a great variety of hors d'oeuvres and other dishes. In Turkey there are special restaurants where only tripe soup and sheep's head are served, all through the day, where people go especially very late at night after a lot of eating and drinking.

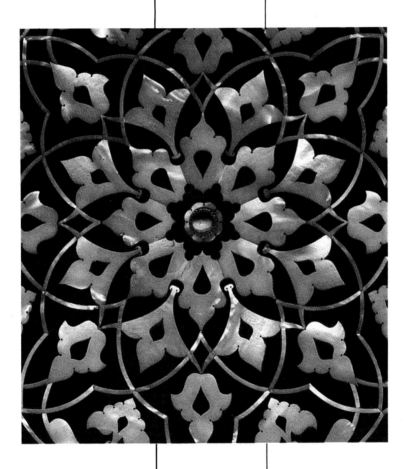

## TARHANA ÇORBASI
### DRIED CURDS SOUP
#### 6 servings

| |
|---|
| 1 glass dried curds with flour (tarhana) |
| 8 glasses meat stock |
| 150 gr. minced meat |
| 6 tablespoons margarine |
| 2 medium size tomatoes or |
| 2 tablespoons tomato paste |
| 2 teaspoons salt |
| 6 slices of bread |

Melt half of the margarine in a large saucepan. Add minced meat and cook until the juice evaporates, stirring from time to time.

Add peeled and chopped tomatoes or tomato paste. Cook for 15 minutes.

Add meat stock and dried curds. Mix well and stir until it starts boiling. Let simmer for 10 minutes.

Serve with diced bread fried in 3 tablespoons of margarine.

## DÜĞÜN ÇORBASI
### WEDDING SOUP
#### 6 servings

| |
|---|
| 500 gr. mutton, cut into small pieces |
| 1 onion |
| 1 carrot |

*Dried curds soup*

*Yoghourt soup*

| ½ tablespoon salt |
| 7 tablespoons margarine |
| 4 tablespoons flour |
| 3 egg yolks |
| Juice of 1 lemon |
| 1 teaspoon ground red pepper |

Put the meat, peeled whole onion and carrot in 3 litres of water. Cover and cook on low heat for 2 hours until the meat is well tender.

Take the meat out and tear it into very small pieces. Put them back into the stock.

Melt 4 tablespoons of margarine in a saucepan. Add the flour and brown it lightly for 2-3 minutes. Slowly add the stock stirring constantly. Pour it into the soup. Cover and let simmer.

Put 3 egg yolks in a bowl. Add the lemon juice and beat well. Go on beating vigorously with a fork, while adding little by little boiling soup with the help of a ladle. Add this mixture to the soup and turn the heat off. Pour it into a soup serving dish.

Heat 3 tablespoons of margarine. Remove from heat and add the red pepper. Pour it over the soup and serve at once.

# YAYLÂ ÇORBASI
## YOGHOURT SOUP
### 6 servings

| 8 glasses meat or chicken stock, or water |
| 80 gr. flour |
| 80 gr. rice |
| 3 glasses yoghourt |
| 2 egg yolks |
| 3 tablespoons butter |
| 2 tablespoons dried mint |

Boil the rice in 8 glasses of meat or chicken broth, on low heat.

Beat the yoghourt with the egg yolks and flour. Stirring constantly, slowly add 2 glasses of boiling stock. Add it to the meat stock with rice. Let simmer for 10 minutes.

Heat the butter. Add dried mint. Leave on low heat for 1 minute. Pour it over the soup and serve.

# UN ÇORBASI
## FLOUR SOUP
### 6 servings

| 8 glasses of meat stock |
| 6 tablespoons butter |
| ¾ glass flour |
| 2 teaspoons salt |
| ⅓ teaspoons ground red pepper |
| 6 slices of bread |
| 6 tablespoons margarine |

Melt 4 tablespoons of butter in a saucepan. Add the flour and lightly brown it. Slowly add the meat stock, stirring constantly, to have a smooth cream. Cover and let simmer for 15 minutes.

Heat 2 tablespoons of butter. Add red pepper and pour over the soup.

Serve with diced bread fried in margarine.

## SÜZME MERCİMEK ÇORBASI
### STRAINED LENTIL SOUP
#### 4 servings

| |
| --- |
| 1 lt. meat stock |
| 125 gr. green lentils |
| 50 gr. flour |
| 2 tablespoons butter |
| Salt and pepper |
| 4-5 slices of stale bread |
| Oil for frying |

*Strained lentil soup*

Pick over and wash lentils, add water to cover and bring to boil. Cover and simmer until the liquid is absorbed. Gradually add the hot meat stock and sieve or put through an electric blender.

Melt the butter, add the flour and stir over medium heat for 1-2 minutes, gradually add the soup. Cover and let simmer for 10 minutes.

Garnish the soup with croutons fried in some oil.

## KIRMIZI MERCİMEK ÇORBASI
### RED LENTIL SOUP

#### 6 servings

| |
| --- |
| 1½ glasses red lentils |
| 8 glasses meat stock |
| 2 medium size onions |
| 2 tablespoons margarine |
| ½ tablespoon flour |
| 1 glass milk |
| 3 egg yolks |
| 1 tablespoon salt |
| ½ teaspoon black pepper |
| 6 slices of bread |
| 3 tablespoons oil |

Wash the red lentils. Put them in 8 glasses of meat stock and 1 glass of plain water. Cook for 35 minutes until they are tender. Pass them through a sieve.

Melt the margarine in another saucepan. Add chopped onions and fry them lightly for 7-8 minutes. Add flour. Brown for 1 minute more. Add them to the meat stock with the lentil purée. Put salt and pepper. Let simmer.

Beat the egg yolks with cold milk. Add to the boiling soup, mix well. Turn the heat off as soon as it starts boiling.

Serve with bread cubes fried in oil.

## PİRİNÇLİ KIRMIZI MERCİMEK ÇORBASI
### RED LENTIL SOUP WITH RICE
#### 4 servings

| |
| --- |
| 1 glass red lentils |
| 2 small onions |
| 2 medium size tomatoes |
| 1 medium size potato |
| 2 tablespoons rice |
| 1 lt. meat stock |
| Salt, pepper |

Wash the lentils and the rice. Add peeled and chopped onions and tomatoes, peeled potato cut into very small cubes and the meat stock. Cover and cook on low heat for 45 minutes.

# EZO GELİN ÇORBASI
## RED LENTILS "BRIDE" SOUP
### 4 servings

| |
|---|
| 100 gr. red lentils |
| 1 onion |
| 1½ lt. water |
| 2 tablespoons tomato paste |
| 100 gr. fine "bulgur" |
| 50 gr. butter |
| ½ teaspoon dried mint |
| Salt, pepper |

Lightly brown the finely chopped onion in butter.

Add the water, washed lentils, "bulgur" (cracked wheat), diluted tomato paste, salt and pepper. Let simmer until the wheat and lentils are very tender.

Sprinkle with red pepper and mint while serving.

## TERBİYELİ ŞEHRİYE ÇORBASI

### VERMICELLI SOUP WITH EGG SAUCE

**4 servings**

| |
|---|
| 1 lt. meat stock or chicken broth |
| 100 gr. vermicelli |
| 1 egg yolk |
| ½ lemon |
| 1 tablespoon butter |
| Salt, paprika |

Add the vermicelli to the boiling stock. Add salt and let simmer until the vermicelli are soft.

Beat the egg yolk with lemon juice. After diluting it with a little of the hot soup, stir it into the pan, stirring all the time. Garnish the soup with melted butter mixed with some paprika.

## ŞEHRİYELİ DOMATES ÇORBASI

### TOMATO SOUP WITH VERMICELLI

**4 servings**

| |
|---|
| 1 lt. meat stock |
| 100 gr. vermicelli |
| 2 tablespoons butter |
| 3 ripe tomatoes |
| 1 bunch parsley |
| Salt, pepper |

Boil the meat stock. Add the vermicelli and the tomatoes, peeled and cut into small pieces. Let simmer for 10 minutes, until the vermicelli are soft.

Garnish with melted butter and chopped parsley.

## PİRİNÇLİ DOMATES ÇORBASI

### TOMATO SOUP WITH RICE

**6 servings**

| |
|---|
| 8 glasses meat stock |
| 4 large tomatoes or |
| 150 gr. tomato paste |
| 1 tablespoon flour |
| 2 tablespoons margarine |
| 65 gr. rice |
| 2 teaspoons salt |

Boil the rice in 2 glasses of water. Drain.

*Tomato soup with vermicelli*

Peel the tomatoes and cut them into small pieces. Melt the margarine. Add the tomatoes or tomato paste dissolved in ½ cup of water. Cook for 15 minutes, stirring from time to time.

Add the flour and salt. Cook for 2 minutes more, stirring constantly. Slowly add the meat stock. Cover and let simmer on low heat for 20 minutes.

Add the rice. Let simmer for 5 minutes more.

## İŞKEMBE ÇORBASI
### TRIPE SOUP
**6 servings**

| |
|---|
| 1 veal tripe (600 gr.) |
| 1 tablespoon salt |
| 2 tablespoons margarine |
| 1 tablespoon flour |
| 2-3 meat stock cubes |
| 2 egg yolks |
| Juice of 1 lemon |
| To serve with: 1 cup vinegar |
| 3 cloves of crushed garlic |
| 3 tablespoons margarine |
| 1 tablespoon ground red pepper |

Clean the tripe well. Wash it thoroughly. Remove the membrane.

Boil it in 3 litres of salted water on low heat, for 4 hours, until it becomes tender. (Take the scum off when it starts boiling.)

Take it out of the water and cut into thin strips. Put them back into the soup. Let simmer.

In a small saucepan, melt the margarine. Add the flour and lightly brown. Stirring constantly, slowly add 6-7 ladles of boiling soup. Add this smooth mixture into the soup, together with 2-3 meat stock cubes. Let simmer for 15 minutes.

In a small bowl, beat the egg yolks with the lemon juice. Slowly add some boiling soup to it. Add this sauce to the soup. When it starts boiling again, turn the heat off.

Serve accompanied with a bowl of vinegar mixed with crushed garlic.

Pour over each individual serving, heated margarine mixed with red pepper.

**MENEMEN**
SCRAMBLED EGGS
WITH VEGETABLES

4 servings

| |
|---|
| 8 eggs |
| 2 green peppers |
| 3 tomatoes |
| 1 teaspoon salt |
| ½ teaspoon pepper |
| 1 tablespoon margarine |

Melt the margarine in a flat pan. Cut seeded peppers into thin rings. Lightly brown them. Add peeled tomatoes cut into small pieces. Cook for 7-8 minutes, stirring from time to time, until the juice half way evaporates.

Beat the eggs in a bowl. Add salt and pepper. Pour into the pan and cook stirring constantly, taking care that it does not get too dry. Serve at once.

## ISPANAKLI YUMURTA
### EGGS ON SPINACH SAUTE
#### 6 servings

| |
|---|
| 12 eggs |
| 1 kg. spinach |
| 2 medium size onions |
| 6 tablespoons margarine |
| 1 teaspoon salt |
| ½ teaspoon pepper |

Remove the roots of the spinach. Cut each stem into two. Wash them well.

Boil 2 lt. of water with some salt. Add the spinach and cook them for 10 minutes.

Drain and chop them.

Melt the margarine. Brown chopped onions. Add the spinach and sauté for 10 minutes. Sprinkle with salt and pepper.

Arrange them in a flat pan. Make 12 hollows and break the eggs into each one. Sprinkle with salt. Cover and cook on medium heat for 3-4 minutes, until the egg whites are cooked.

Serve at once.

## ÇILBIR
### POACHED EGGS WITH YOGHOURT
**4 servings**

| |
|---|
| 8 very fresh eggs |
| 2 tablespoons salt |
| 2½ tablespoons vinegar |
| 500 gr. yoghourt |
| 2 cloves of garlic |
| 3 tablespoons margarine |
| 1 teaspoon ground red pepper |

Beat the yoghourt with some salt and crushed garlics.

Fill a large and flat pan ¾ full with water. Add salt and vinegar. Let boil.

Lower the heat. Break each egg first into a small plate, then slide it slowly into the gently boiling water. Cook for 3 minutes and take it out with a skimmer. Drain well. Repeat the same with all the eggs and arrange them in a serving dish.

Cover them with yoghourt.

Heat the margarine. Remove from heat and add red pepper. Pour it over the yoghourt and serve immediately.

*Poached eggs with yoghourt*

There is a great variety of hors d'oeuvres (called "meze") which are especially fit for a "rakı" table (a strong alcoholic drink made of aniseed and grapes). In Turkey, drinking "rakı" is almost a ritual: a friendly gathering during which you take your time over many different "mezes" in small quantities, starting with cold and simple ones such as white cheese and salads, finishing off with warm ones like fried pastries or croquettes. Then you can have the main dish, which is usually fish or broiled meat. However, it happens that with so many different kinds of delicious "mezes" you are already full and don't have a chance to pass on to the main dish!

## ÇİĞ KÖFTE
### RAW MEATBALLS
**8 servings**

| |
|---|
| 1 kg. minced lean meat (not very fresh meat, specially cut and minced 4-5 times for ''çiğ köfte'') |
| 1 kg. fine ''bulgur'' (boiled and pounded wheat) |
| 2 large onions, grated |
| 1 dozen cloves of garlic, crushed |
| 1 tablespoon cummin |
| 1 tablespoon pepper |
| 1 cup hot red pepper paste |
| ½ cup tomato paste |
| 1 tablespoon olive oil |
| Garnish: 1 bunch of green onions |
| 1 bunch of parsley |
| 1 teaspoon ground red pepper |
| ½ teaspoon salt |
| Juice of ½ lemon |
| 1 tablespoon olive oil |
| Cos lettuce leaves |

Pour 1 glass of hot water over the ''bulgur'' and let stand. (You may replace the hot water with 1 glass of grated tomatoes.)

Mix the meat with the other ingredients and leave for 1 hour.

Mix the meat with the ''bulgur'' and vigorously knead for 20 minutes, rubbing it against the side of your hand.

Take small walnut size pieces of it and squeezing each one in the palm of your hand give it an irregular shape. Arrange them on a serving dish.

Serve with cos lettuce leaves and a mixture of chopped green onions and parsley with salt, red pepper, lemon and olive oil.

## PATLICAN VE BİBER TAVA
### FRIED EGG-PLANTS AND
### BELL PEPPERS
**6 servings**

| |
|---|
| 1 kg. medium size egg-plants |
| 6 bell peppers |
| 1 tablespoon salt |
| 1½ glasses oil |
| Sauce: 3 large tomatoes |
| 4 cloves of garlic |
| 2 tablespoons vinegar |
| Salt, pepper |
| or |
| 500 gr. yoghourt |
| 4 cloves of garlic |

Remove the stems of the egg-plants. Without peeling, cut them lengthwise into ½ cm. thick slices, or peel them leaving lenthwise stripes and cut them diagonally into 1 cm. thick slices. Sprinkle with salt and let stand for 20 minutes.

Heat the oil in a frying pan. Dry the egg-plant slices pressing lightly. Fry them until golden brown on both sides. Drain well. Arrange on a serving dish.

Cut seeded bell peppers into halves. Lightly brown them in tha same frying pan. Arrange them on the egg-plant slices.

Serve cool, either with tomato sauce or yoghourt beaten with crushed garlic and salt.

Tomato sauce: Reduce the oil in the pan. Add peeled and chopped tomatoes and crushed garlic. Cook on medium heat for 7-8 minutes, stirring from time to time. Add salt, pepper and vinegar. Mix well and pour over the fried egg-plants and bell peppers.

## KABAK SALATASI
### ZUCCHINI SQUASH SALAD
**6 servings**

| |
|---|
| 1 kg. medium size zucchini squash |
| 250 gr. yoghourt |
| 2 cloves of garlic, crushed |
| 1 teaspoon salt |
| 1 bunch of dill |
| 5-6 black olives |

Grate and cut the squash into pieces. Boil in salted water until they are well tender. Drain well and press lightly on them to extract all the water.

Put them in a bowl and mash with a fork. Add yoghourt, garlic, salt and chopped dill. Decorate with olives.

## MERCİMEK KÖFTESİ
### RED LENTIL BALLS
**6 servings**

| |
|---|
| 1 glass red lentils |
| 1 glass fine "bulgur" |
| (boiled and pounded wheat) |
| ½ glass oil |
| 1 medium size onion |
| 1 tablespoon tomato paste |
| 1 teaspoon salt |
| 1 teaspoon ground red pepper |
| 1 teaspoon cummin |
| 1 bunch of parsley |
| 6-7 fresh green onions |
| Cos lettuce leaves |

Wash the lentils and cook them in 3-4 glasses of water.

Just before the whole water is absorbed, add the "bulgur". Boil for 1-2 minutes. Turn the heat off and let stand for 20 minutes.

Brown finely chopped onion in oil. Add the tomato paste and remove from heat.

Add the browned onions, spices and finely chopped spring onions and parsley to the lentils with "bulgur". Mix well. Let cool.

Take small walnut size pieces of it and squeezing in the palm of your hand shape them irregularly.

Arrange them on a layer of cos lettuce leaves and serve.

## ÇOBAN SALATASI
### SHEPHERD'S SALAD
**4 servings**

| 2 large tomatoes |
| 1 mild onion |
| 3 medium size sweet peppers |
| 1 medium size cucumber |
| ½ bunch parsley |
| Olive oil |
| Lemon |
| Salt |

Slice the onion.

Dice the tomatoes.

Peel and cut the cucumber in small pieces.

Remove the stalks and seeds of the peppers and dice.

Coarsely chop the parsley.

Mix everything together and sprinkle with salt.

Garnish with olive oil and lemon juice.

## YOĞURTLU HAVUÇ KIZARTMASI
### FRIED CARROTS WITH YOGHURT
**6 servings**

| 1½ kg. large carrots |
| --- |
| 300 gr. flour |
| 1½ glass oil |
| 500 gr. yoghourt |
| Salt |

Boil 10 glasses of water in a saucepan.

Scrape the carrots and cut them lengthwise into thin slices of 3-4 mm. Cook them in boiling water until they start to get soft. Drain and let cool.

Put the flour and 1 teaspoon of salt in a flat bowl. Slowly add 5½ cups of water, stirring constantly, until it becomes smooth and creamy.

Heat the oil in a frying pan. Dip the carrot slices one by one into the flour paste and fry them in oil until they are golden brown on both sides (not more than 4-5 at a time).

Serve with salted yoghourt.

## YOĞURTLU HAVUÇ
### CARROTS WITH YOGHOURT
**4 servings**

| ½ kg. carrots |
| --- |
| 2 tablespoons olive oil |
| 250 gr. yoghourt |
| 2 cloves of garlic |
| Salt, paprika |

Scrape and coarsely grate the carrots. Sauté in olive oil with some salt.

Whip the yoghourt with crushed garlic. Add to the carrots. Mix well. Sprinkle with paprika.

*Carrots with yoghourt*

## YOĞURTLU PATLICAN SALATASI

### EGG-PLANT SALAD WITH YOGHOURT

**4 servings**

| |
|---|
| **6 large egg-plants** |
| **Juice of one lemon** |
| **2 tablespoons olive oil** |
| **1 teaspoon salt** |
| **2 cloves of garlic** |
| **½ glass yoghourt** |
| **1 tomato** |
| **1 bell pepper** |
| **A few black olives** |

Proceed the same way as described for egg-plant salad in the following recipe.

To the mashed egg-plants, add salt, crushed garlic and yoghourt. Mix well.

Arrange on a dish. Decorate with slices of tomatoes, green pepper and black olives.

## PATLICAN SALATASI

### EGG-PLANT SALAD

**4 servings**

| |
|---|
| **6 large egg-plants** |
| **Juice of 1 lemon** |
| **½ cup olive oil** |
| **1 tablespoon vinegar** |
| **2 tomatoes** |
| **1 onion** |
| **6 green peppers** |
| **1 dozen black olives** |

Put the lemon juice and olive oil in a bowl.

Grill whole egg-plants on gas flame (or wood fire) until they are burnt outside and very soft inside.

Hold each egg-plant by the stem under running tap water for 2-3 seconds. Then peel the skin off with a knife. Cut the stem off and mash it with a fork. Put it immediately in the bowl, mixing well with lemon juice and olive oil.

Add vinegar and salt. Mix well. Arrange on a serving dish. Decorate with peeled and sliced tomatoes, sliced peppers, finely sliced onion and black olives.

*Egg-plants salad*

## EZME
### CRUSHED TOMATO SALAD
**6 servings**

| |
|---|
| 250 gr. ripe tomatoes |
| 1 sweet green pepper |
| ½ cucumber |
| 2 spring onions |
| 1 teaspoon dried mint |
| Salt, pepper, paprika |
| 1 tablespoon paprika paste |
| 1 tablespoon olive oil |
| 2 tablespoons vinegar |

Peel the tomatoes and the cucumber. Remove the stalk and seeds of the pepper. Remove the outer layer of the spring onions.

Chop them up very small, without actually pulverising them.

Add all the other ingredients. Mix well.

*Crushed tomato salad*

## HUMUS
### CHICK-PEAS PASTE
**4 servings**

| |
|---|
| 1½ glasses chick-peas |
| ½ glass ground sesame seed (tahin) |
| ½ glass olive oil |
| 1½ teaspoons salt |
| 1½ teaspoons ground red pepper |
| 4 cloves of garlic |
| Juice of 2-3 lemons |

Soak the chick-peas in water overnight. Change the water and cook until they are well tender. Remove the skins and mash.

Add "tahin", crushed garlic, salt and pepper. Mix well. Slowly add olive oil and lemon juice to make a smooth paste.

Arrange on a serving dish. Serve with toasted bread.

*White beans salad*

## FASULYE PİYAZI
### WHITE BEANS SALAD
**4 servings**

| |
|---|
| **250 gr. white beans** |
| **1 glass vinegar** |
| **1 large onion** |
| **3 tomatoes** |
| **3 bell peppers** |
| **1 dozen black olives** |
| **½ bunch of parsley** |
| **3 hard boiled eggs** |
| **2 teaspoons salt** |
| **⅓ glass olive oil.** |

Soak the beans in water overnight. Drain and put them in boiling water. Cook on medium heat until they are tender.

Drain and put the beans in a bowl. Sprinkle with some salt and pour over them ¾ glass of vinegar. Leave for 2-3 hours.

Cut the onions into lengthwise slices. Put them in a bowl, rub them with some salt to extract the juice. Wash and drain them.

Drain the beans. Add the onions and chopped parsley. Mix well. Arrange on a serving dish.

Cut the bell peppers into slices. Peel the tomatoes and cut them into pieces. Slice the hard boiled eggs.

Decorate the beans with peppers, tomatoes, eggs and olives.

Mix in a small bowl olive oil, salt and the rest of the vinegar. Pour over the beans.

## PATLICAN KÖFTESİ
### EGG-PLANT FINGERS
**6 servings**

| |
|---|
| **1 kg. large egg-plants** |
| **50 gr. grated cheese** |
| **3 eggs** |
| **1½ tablespoons flour** |
| **1 bunch of parsley** |
| **1 glass oil** |
| **Sauce: 3 tablespoons margarine** |
| **2 tablespoons flour** |
| **1½ glasses milk** |
| **2 teaspoons salt** |
| **1 small lemon** |

Grill whole egg-plants on gas flame until burnt outside and very soft inside. Holding from the stem, peel each one lengthwise with a knife. Put them in 4 glasses of water with lemon juice.

Melt the margarine in a saucepan. Add the flour and brown for 2 minutes. Slowly add warm milk, stirring constantly. Cook for 1-2 minutes and turn the heat off.

Add grated cheese, salt, chopped parsley and squeezed egg-plants. Mix well, mashing with a fork. Let stand in the refrigerator for 2 hours.

Heat the oil. Beat the eggs in a bowl. Take big walnut size pieces of the egg-plant paste and roll each one in the palms of your hands to shape them like fingers. Dip them first into some flour, then in beaten eggs. Fry them until golden brown. Drain well.

## PATATES KÖFTESİ
### POTATO CROQUETTES
**6 servings**

| | |
|---|---|
| **1 kg. fresh potatoes** | |
| **200 gr. grated cheese** | |
| **or 250 gr. mashed white cheese** | |
| **2 tablespoons flour** | |
| **3 eggs** | |
| **2 teaspoons salt** | |
| **½ teaspoon pepper** | |
| **1½ glasses oil** | |

Boil unpeeled potatoes for 25-30 minutes. Drain, peel and mash them.

While they are hot, add cheese, flour, eggs, salt and pepper. Mix well and knead to make a consistent paste.

Take big walnut size pieces of this paste and in the palms of your hands roll them into finger shapes. Arrange them on a tray sprinkled with flour.

Heat the oil in a frying pan. Fry them until golden brown.

## DOLDURULMUŞ BİBER TURŞUSU
### PICKLED STUFFED PEPPERS

| | |
|---|---|
| **1 kg. green bell peppers** | |
| **1 small white cabbage** | |
| **2 sweet red peppers** | |
| **1 bulb of garlic** | |
| **1 bunch of parsley** | |
| **10-12 green springs of celery** | |
| **2 cups of vinager** | |
| **Salt (1 tablespoonful to each** | |
| **4½ cups of water)** | |

Remove the stalks and seeds from the peppers.

Finely chop the cabbage, red peppers,

garlic, parsley and celery stalks. Mix them well.

Stuff the peppers with this mixture and arrange in a pickle jar.

Pour over water mixed with salt and vinager.

Let stand for about three weeks.

# FAVA

## FAVA BEANS PUREE

### 6 servings

| |
|---|
| 2 glasses fava beans |
| 1 large onion |
| ¼ glass olive oil |
| 2 teaspoons salt |
| 4 teaspoons sugar |
| ½ bunch of dill or parsley |
| 1 lemon |

Soak the dry fava beans in water overnight. Drain and put them in a saucepan. Add the onion, peeled and cut into four pieces, olive oil, salt, sugar and enough water to cover them.

Cover and cook on medium heat until the beans are well tender(20 minutes in pressure cooker).

Mash them while still hot and make a smooth and not very thick purée.

Pour it into a flat bowl. Let cool and get hard. Turn it upside down onto a serving dish. Decorate with dill or parsley leaves. Serve with slices of lemon.

*Fried liver*

## ARNAVUT CİĞERİ
### FRIED LIVER
**4 servings**

| |
|---|
| 1 sheep liver or 2 lamb livers |
| ½ cup flour |
| 2 teaspoons red ground pepper |
| 1 teaspoon salt |
| 1 glass oil |
| 3 medium size onions |
| 1 bunch parsley |

Cut the onions in half and each half into thin lengthwise slices. Put them in a bowl and rub with 1 teaspoon of salt to extract the juice. Wash and drain. Add chopped parsley. Leave it aside to be used as garnish for the livers.

Remove the membrane and the veins of the liver. Cut it into small cubes, the size of a large hazelnut. Wash and drain well.

Add 1 teaspoon of red pepper.

Heat the olive oil in a frying pan. Take a handful of liver cubes, coat them with flour and fry in very hot olive oil for one minute. Take them out and repeat the same with the rest of the liver cubes. Sprinkle with ½ teaspoon of salt.

Serve accompanied with the garnish.

## KISIR
### "BULGUR" SALAD
**6 servings**

| |
|---|
| 1 glass fine "bulgur" |
| (boiled and pounded wheat) |
| 3 tablespoons hot red pepper paste |
| 1 tomato, peeled and finely chopped |
| 6 fresh green onions, finely chopped |
| 1 bunch of parsley, finely chopped |
| 2 teaspoons salt |
| 2 teaspoons dried mint |
| ¼ glass olive oil |
| ¼ glass vinegar |

Put the "bulgur" in a bowl. Pour over it boiling water, just enough to cover it. Cover the bowl well with a lid and let stand until the water is absorbed and the "bulgur" grains are swollen.

Add all the other ingredients. Mix well and serve.

## BEYİN SALATASI
### BRAIN SALAD
**6 servings**

| |
|---|
| 4 lamb brains |
| 4 tablespoons olive oil |
| 1 lemon |
| ½ cup vinegar |
| 1 small onion |
| 1 teaspoon salt |
| Parsley |

Soak the brains in cold water and leave for one hour, changing the water 2-3 times.

Remove the membranes under running water.

Put the brains in 6 glasses of cold water. Add some salt, vinegar and the onion cut into four pieces. Cover and cook on medium heat for 10 minutes.

Let them cool. Place the brains on a serving plate. Sprinkle with olive oil and lemon juice. Decorate with parsley leaves.

# CACIK
## YOGHOURT WITH CUCUMBERS
(Pronounced as "jajik")
**4 servings**

| |
|---|
| **500 gr. yoghourt** |
| **2 medium size cucumbers** |
| **1 teaspoon salt** |
| **2-3 sprigs of dill** |
| **1 teaspoon dried mint** |
| **1 clove of crushed garlic (optional)** |
| **2 tablespoons olive oil (optional)** |

Peel the cucumbers and cut them into very small and thin pieces. Sprinkle with salt and leave aside.

Put the yoghourt in a bowl. Beat it well with a fork or a whisk, slowly adding up to one cup of water.

Add the salted cucumbers and crushed garlic. Sprinkle with chopped dill and dried mint. Slowly pour the oil over it.

Serve chilled.

## ÇERKEZ TAVUĞU
### CIRCASSIAN CHICKEN
**6 servings**

| |
|---|
| 1 chicken (1000-1200 gr.) |
| 1 small onion |
| 1 small carrot |
| ½ tablespoon salt |
| Sauce: 400 gr. walnuts |
| 3 thin slices of dry bread |
| (without crust) |
| 1 teaspoon ground red pepper |

*Circassian chicken*

| |
|---|
| 2-3 cloves of garlic |
| 3 glasses chicken stock |

Put a peeled whole onion, grated carrot, cleaned and washed chicken and salt into a saucepan. Cover with water. Cover and cook on low heat until tender.

Let cool. Take the chicken out of its stock. Remove the skin and bones, tear it into small pieces.

Grind the walnuts. Soak the bread in water. Squeeze them to extract the water. Crumble and add to the ground walnuts together with crushed garlic and red pep-

per. Put the mixture through a food mill and add the chicken broth to make a creamy sauce which should not be too thick. (All the ingredients for the sauce may also be blended in an electric blender.)

Pour half of the sauce on the chicken pieces. Mix well. Arrange them on a serving dish. Spread the rest of the sauce over. Decorate with thin lines of ground red pepper. Serve cool.

## PATLICAN BÖREĞİ
### EGG-PLANT PASTIES
**4 servings**

| |
|---|
| **3 large egg-plants** |
| **1 tablespoon salt** |
| **Filling: 350 gr. white cheese** |
| **3 eggs** |
| **1 bunch of parsley** |
| **For frying: 2 eggs** |
| **250 gr. fine bread crumbs** |
| **1½ glasses oil** |

Cut the egg-plants lengthwise inte ½ cm. thick slices. Then cut each slice into three. Sprinkle with salt and let stand for 20 minutes.

Heat the oil. Wash and dry the egg-plant slices. Fry them lightly brown on both sides. Let cool.

Mash the white cheese with a fork. Add the eggs and chopped parsley. Mix well to make a paste.

Put a small amount of this paste on half of the egg-plant slices, covering each one with another slice and pressing lightly to stick them together.

Beat 2 eggs. Dip the egg-plants first into the eggs, then in bread crumbs. Fry them for 4-5 minutes until golden brown on both sides. Drain well.

Various kinds of pastries, called "börek", constitute an important part in Turkish cookery. Different sorts of dough can be prepared at home, but it is also a great facility to buy ready made thin sheets of dough (philo dough), called "yufka".

The "börek" can be prepared with different kinds of fillings and can be baked or fried.

## BOHÇA BÖREĞİ
### FLAKY PASTRY-I
**6 servings**

| |
|---|
| **400 gr. flour** |
| **330 gr. melted butter** |
| **1 tablespoon salt** |
| **1 tablespoon lemon juice** |
| **1 egg yolk** |
| **½ cup olive oil** |
| **Desired filling (page 35,38)** |

Sift 350 gr. of flour. Make a hollow in the middle. Put 1 tablespoon of melted butter, salt, lemon juice and ¾ cup of water. Mix and knead to make a soft dough. Cover it with a wet cloth and leave for half an hour.

Sprinkle the table top and the dough with flour. With a rolling pin, roll it out to make a disc of about ½ cm. thick and 30-40 cm. wide.

Spread the melted butter on both sides of the disc. Fold it in three, then fold this long dough in three again. Cover it with a wet cloth and let stand for 45-60 minutes.

Roll it out again to make a thin disc. Fold it the same way as before. Cover and let stand for another 45 minutes.

Roll it out again, this time about 2 cm. thick. Cut out strips of 3-4 cm. wide, then cut the strips into 3-4 cm. pieces. Roll each piece in the palms of the hands to make small balls. Let stand for 15 minutes.

Prepare the desired filling.

Take each ball, dip it into olive oil. With the rolling pin, roll it out into a square shape as thin as possible. Put in the middle of it 1 tablespoon of the desired filling. Fold the four corners onto it. Place it on a slightly wet oven pan.

Beat the egg yolk with 1 teaspoon olive oil and 1 tablespoon of water. Spread it with a brush on the pastries.

Bake them in the oven for 25-30 minutes, until they are golden brown.

## SİGARA VE MUSKA BÖREĞİ
### CIGARETTE "BÖREK" AND
### TRIANGULAR "BÖREK"
**4 servings**

| |
|---|
| **3 sheets of "yufka" (philo dough)** |
| **1 glass oil** |
| **Minced meat or white cheese filling** |

Prepare the desired filling (see page 35 ).

To make cigarette "böreks":

Put the "yufkas" one on top of the other. Fold them in half and cut along the diameter. Then cut these semi-circular layers into four equal parts. Thus you will have 24 equal triangular sheets.

On the shorter end of each triangle put a small amount of the desired filling. Fold the two sides over and roll it on like a cigarette. Dip the sharp end in a glass of water and stick it on.

To make triangular ones, called "amulet börek":

Put the "yufkas" one on top of the other. Fold them in half and cut along the diameter. Then cut these semi-circular layers into strips of 7-8 cm. wide and 22-24 cm. long.

On one end of each strip, put a small amount of the desired filling. Take the right corner of the strip and fold it diagonally over the filling to form a triangle. Then take the left corner and fold it on. Continue until the end of the strip, thus forming a small triangular parcel. Stick the end with water.

Heat the oil in a frying pan. Fry them on medium heat, until they are golden brown on both sides. Drain well. Serve hot.

## MANTI
### MEAT PASTIES
**6 servings**

| |
|---|
| **Dough: 400 gr. flour** |
| **1 egg yolk** |
| **1 whole egg** |
| **½ tablespoon salt** |
| **100 gr. water** |
| **Filling: 200 gr. minced meat** |
| **3 medium size oinons** |
| **Salt, pepper** |
| **For boiling: 6 glasses meat stock** |
| **To serve with: 500 gr. yoghourt** |
| **2-3 cloves of garlic** |
| **5 tablespoons margarine** |
| **1 tablespoon ground red pepper** |
| **1 tablespoon dried mint (optional)** |

Mix the minced meat with grated onions, salt and pepper. Knead for 2 minutes.

Sift 350 gr. of flour. Make a hollow in the middle. Put 1 whole egg, 1 egg yolk, ½ tablespoon of salt and 100 gr. water. Mix well and knead to make a smooth dough. Cover it with a wet cloth and leave for 1 hour.

Sprinkle the table top with flour. Place the dough. Sprinkle it with flour also. With a rolling pin, roll it out to the size of a plate. Then, with a thin rolling pin (*oklava*), make it bigger and as thin as possible.

Cut out 6 cm. squares and into each one put 1 teaspoon of meat filling. Bring the four corners of the dough together and squeezing with the fingers, stick them together. Arrange them in an oven pan brushed with melted margarine.

*Meat pasties*

Bake them in medium hot oven for 25 minutes, until they are lightly browned. Pour over them 6 glasses of hot meat stock. Cover and cook in the oven or on low heat until the whole stock is absorbed and the pasties are well cooked.

Share them out on individual plates. Spread over them yoghourt beaten with crushed garlic and some salt. Pour over margarine, heated and mixed with red pepper. Sprinkle with dried mint.

Serve at once.

## PEYNİRLİ BÖREK İÇİ
### CHEESE FILLING FOR PASTRIES

| |
| --- |
| **200 gr. white skim cheese** |
| **1 whole egg or 1 egg white** |
| **½ bunch of parsley** |
| **½ bunch of dill (optional)** |

Mash the white cheese with a fork. Add the egg and chopped parsley and dill. Mix well.

## KIYMALI BÖREK İÇİ
### MINCED MEAT FILLING FOR PASTRIES
**1 servings**

| |
| --- |
| **150 gr. minced meat** |
| **3 medium size onions** |
| **1½ tablespoons margarine** |
| **½ bunch of parsley** |
| **Salt, pepper** |

Brown chopped onions lightly in margarine.

Add the meat and salt. Cook it stirring constantly until the juice evaporates.

Add salt, pepper and chopped parsley. Mix well.

## KIYMALI PİDE
### MEAT PIZZA
**6 servings**

| |
|---|
| **5 cups flour** |
| **4 tablespoons butter** |
| **2 teaspoons yeast** |
| **2 tablespoons milk** |
| **1 teaspoon salt** |
| **1 teaspoon sugar** |
| **3 eggs (separate 1 yolk for brushing on top)** |
| **250 gr. minced lamb** |
| **½ bunch of parsley** |
| **1 medium size onion** |
| **Salt, pepper** |

Dissolve the yeast and sugar in the milk.

Sieve the flour in a bowl, make a hole in the middle and into this place the yeast, the softened butter, 2 eggs and salt. Knead into a soft dough, cover and set aside to rise.

Divide the dough into egg-size pieces and on a floured board flatten each with the hands into a circular or eliptical shape about half a centimetre thick.

Meat pizza

Prepare the meat filling (p. 35) and spread down the centre of each piece of pastry. Fold the edges inwards about 2 cm. so that the filling can be seen.

Leave in a warm place to rise again. Brush with egg yolk and bake in a moderate oven until they are golden brown.

Brush lightly with melted butter and serve immediately if you want them crispy. Otherwise, keep covered in a saucepan for about 5 minutes.

## TATAR BÖREĞI
### TARTAR MEAT PASTIES
**6 servings**

| Dough: 400 gr. flour |
| --- |
| 75 cl. milk |
| 2 eggs |
| ½ tablespoon salt |
| Filling: 200 gr. minced meat |
| 1½ tablespoons margarine |
| 3 medium size onions |
| 1 teaspoon salt |
| ½ teaspoon pepper |
| ½ bunch of parsley |
| Sauce: 500 gr. yoghourt |
| 2-3 cloves of garlic |
| 1 teaspoon salt |
| To serve with: 4 tablespoons butter |
| 1 teaspoon ground red pepper |

Sift 350 gr. flour. Make a hollow in the middle. Put the eggs, salt and milk. Mix well and knead to make a consistent dough. Cover it with a wet cloth and let stand for 1 hour.

Prepare the meat filling as described on (page 35).

Sprinkle the table top and the dough with flour. With a rolling pin, roll it out to make a plate size disc. Then, with a thin rolling pin (oklava), roll it out to make it as big and thin as possible.

On one side of the dough, put small amounts of filling, 5-6 cm. apart from one another. Fold the edge over, press lightly and with the edge of a small plate cut out crescents. Bring the two ends of each crescent together and press to stick them together. Proceed the same way for the whole dough. Place them on a tray sprinkled with flour.

Boil 3 litres of salted water in a large saucepan. Drop the pasties in and boil for 10 minutes until they are soft.

Take them out with a skimmer and drain well. Share them out in individual plates. Cover with yoghourt beaten with crushed garlic and salt. Pour some heated butter mixed red pepper. Serve at once.

## TEPSI BÖREĞI
### BAKED "BÖREK"
**6 servings**

| 3 sheets of "yufka" (philo dough) |
| --- |
| ¾ glass milk |
| 6 tablespoons margarine |
| 2 eggs |
| Desired filling (minced meat, white cheese or spinach |

Brush an oven pan of 24-30 cm. in diameter with melted margarine. Add the eggs and milk to the rest of the melted margarine and beat them well.

Lay one sheet of "yufka" into the pan, allowing the edges to go 8-10 cm. beyond the rims. Tear the excess parts away.

Spread 3-4 tablespoonful of the milk mixture over the "yufka".

Lay two more layers of "yufka", cut the same size as the pan, spreading milk mixture on each layer.

Spread the desired filling (page 35,38) Lay the rest of the "yufka" in 2-3 layers, always moistening them with the milk mixture. Fold the edges of the first "yufka" over. Spread the remaining milk mixture all over it.

Bake in medium hot oven for 25-30 minutes until it is golden brown.

## ISPANAKLI BÖREK İÇİ
### SPINACH FILLING FOR PASTRIES

| |
|---|
| **1250 gr. spinach** |
| **3 medium size onions** |
| **6 tablespoons margarine** |
| **1 teaspoon salt** |
| **½ teaspoon pepper** |

Remove the roots of the spinach, wash them well.

Put them in a saucepan, cover with water, boil at high temperature for 5 minutes.

Drain and squeeze by hand to extract excess water. Chop them with a knife.

38

*Baked "börek"*

Melt the margarine in a saucepan. Add chopped onions and salt. Brown them lightly. Add the chopped spinach and cook for 10 minutes stirring constantly. Add some pepper.

## ERİŞTE
### HOME-MADE NOODLES

This homemade strip pasta is common in the provinces and can be purchased dried in city supermarkets.

| |
|---|
| **1 kg flour** |
| **5 eggs** |
| **½ cup water or milk** |
| **salt** |

Sieve the flour onto a pastry board, make a dip in the centre and into this break 5 whole eggs, 2 teaspoons of salt, and half a cup of water or milk, and knead very well. The dough will be fairly stiff and when cut no small air bubbles should be visible.

Divide the dough into two equal parts, cover with a damp cloth and set aside for 20 minutes.

Roll out each piece into regular circles 2-3 mm in thickness.

Leave the rolled out pastry on a floured board until it is partially dried (about 1½ hours).

Cut into quarter circles and stack one on top of the other, flouring each piece, and cut these into strips about 3 cm wide, then cut the strips widthways into pieces 3-4 mm wide so that each piece is the size of a match.

Spread the pieces on a clean dry cloth and leave to dry in a cool place. When they are completely dry, pack in boxes or bags.

## PEYNİRLİ ERİŞTE
### HOME-MADE NOODLES
### WITH CHEESE

This recipe uses the homemade erishte described in the above recipe.

| |
|---|
| **500 gm erishte** |
| **3 eggs** |
| **100 gm cheese** |
| **(yellow kaşar or white feta)** |
| **1 litre milk** |
| **2 tblsp butter** |
| **salt and pepper** |

Put the milk, 3 cups of water and 2 teaspoons of salt in a saucepan and bring to the boil.

Toss in the erishte and boil until the pasta is tender. Drain.

Add half of the grated cheese and butter and stir well, then empty into an oven dish. Sprinkle the remainder of the cheese on top and bake in the oven until the cheese is golden brown.

## SU BÖREĞİ
### WATER PASTRY
**6 servings**

| |
|---|
| **350 gr. flour** |
| **2 tablespoons water** |
| **3 eggs** |
| **1 tablespoon salt** |
| **100 gr. starch** |
| **6 tablespoons margarine** |
| **Meat filling: 200 gr. minced lean meat** |
| **2 tablespoons margarine** |
| **3 onions** |
| **½ bunch of parsley** |
| **1 teaspoon salt** |
| **½ teaspoon pepper** |
| **Cheese filling:** |
| **250 gr. mashed white cheese** |
| **1 egg** |
| **½ cup milk** |
| **½ bunch of dill** |
| **½ bunch of parsley** |

Sift 350 gr. of flour. Make a hollow in the middle. Put the eggs, water and salt. Mix and knead. Divide into 9 pieces (one of them bigger than the other 8). Flatten each piece. Cover them with a damp cloth and let stand for half an hour.

Prepare the desired filling (page 35 ).

With a rolling pin, roll out the bigger piece of dough twice as big as the baking pan, which should be a straight-sided one of 25 cm. in diameter. Place the rolled out dough into the buttered pan, with the edges coming out of the pan.

Roll the other 8 pieces out. Put 4 of them together, one on top of the other, sprinkling with starch between each layer. Roll them out together, as big as the baking pan. Repeat the same for the other 4.

Boil 4 litres of water with 1½ tablespoons of salt. Boil the doughs one by one for 1 minute each. Take them out, taking care not to tear them, dip in a bowl of cold water, drain and place into the baking pan, with melted margarine in between.

After 4 layers of dough, spread the desired filling. Put the other 4 layers of dough, boiled one by one. Fold the edges of the first one over. Spread on the remaining margarine.

Bake in medium hot oven for 1½ hours, until golden brown.

Take it out of the oven and put it upside down on a round serving dish. Serve at once.

## PUF BÖREĞİ
### PUFF PASTRIES
#### 6 servings

| |
|---|
| 350 gr. flour |
| 1 tablespoon margarine |
| 2½ taslespoons butter |
| ¾ tablespoon salt |
| 1 egg yolk |
| Meat filling: 200 gr. minced meat |
| 3 onions (chopped) |
| 1½ tablespoons margarine |
| 1 teaspoon salt |
| ½ teaspoon pepper |
| Cheese filling: 200 gr. white cheese (mashed) |
| 1 egg white |
| 1 bunch of parsley |
| For frying: 1½ glasses oil |

Sift 350 gr. of flour. Make a hollow in the middle. Put the egg yolk, melted margarine, salt and ½ cup of water. Mix and knead to make a soft dough (as soft as the ear lobe). Cover with a wet cloth and let stand for 1 hour.

Sprinkle the table top with flour. Divide the dough into 5 equal pieces. With a rolling pin, roll each one out to a plate size disc. Spread melted butter on each one and place them one on top of the other. Cover with a damp cloth. Let stand in a cool place for 1 hour.

Prepare the desired filling.

Roll the doughs out, all together, as big and thin as possible. On one side of the dough, put small amounts of the filling. Fold the edge over and press lightly. Cut out crescents and make sure that the edges are well sealed.

*Puff pastries*

Place them in a tray sprinkled with flour. Proceed the same way until you finish the whole dough.

Heat the oil in a frying pan. Fry the pastries (3-4 at a time) until golden brown on both sides, pouring spoonfuls of the same hot oil over while frying. Drain well and arrange on a serving dish. Serve at once.

## ÇİĞ BÖREK
### RAW PASTRY
**6 servings**

| |
|---|
| ½ kg. flour |
| 1 egg |
| 1 teaspoon salt |
| Filling: 600 gr. minced lean meat |
| 2 tomatoes |
| 1 medium size onion |
| 2 green peppers |
| Salt, pepper |
| Oil for frying |

Sift the flour. Make hollow in the middle. Put the egg and salt. Slowly adding some water make a smooth dough. Knead for 5 minutes. Cover and leave aside.

Mix the minced meat with grated tomatoes, grated onion, finely sliced green peppers, salt, pepper and ½ cup of water (if it is too thick).

Take egg size pieces from the dough. Roll each one in the palms of the hands into balls. With a rolling pin, roll them out to 15 cm. discs. Heap them up in layers with sheets of paper in between.

Heat the frying pan with oil in it. (It can either be 1 glass of oil in which the "böreks" will be deep-fried, or just enough oil to wet a non-stick (teflon) frying pan in which the "böreks" will be toasted, the latter being lighter.)

Take a sheet of dough. Put a thin layer of filling in half of it. Fold the other half over and pressing with fingers stick the edges well.

Fry them lightly brown on both sides (2 at a time in the frying pan). (Fill the "böreks" just before frying them. Do not let them stand already filled, otherwise the juice of the filling will spoil the dough.)

## NEMSE BÖREĞİ
### FLAKY PASTRY-II
**6 servings**

| |
|---|
| 350 gr. flour |
| 1½ tablespoons softened margarine |
| 320 gr. margarine |
| ¾ glass water |
| 1 tablespoon salt |
| 1 teaspoon lemon juice or vinegar |
| To roll out: 100 gr. flour |
| Desired filling (page 35,38) |

Sift the flour (preferably on a marble or tile top table). Make a hollow in the middle. Put softened margarine, lemon juice or vinegar, salt. Slowly add water. Mix well and knead for 10 minutes. Make a ball and wrap it into wax-paper. Let stand in a cool place for half an hour.

Sprinkle the table top and the dough with flour. With a rolling pin, roll it out to make a ½ cm. thick star with 4 corners. In the center, place a 320 gr. piece of margarine (hard, not softened) and fold the corners over. Wrap it up again with wax-paper and leave in the refrigerator for 1 hour.

Place it on floured table top. With the rolling pin, roll it out into a ½ cm. thick long piece. Fold the two ends towards the center, then fold it again like a wallet. Roll it out again and fold it again into four. Wrap it up and leave in the refrigerator for 1 hour more.

Repeat this rolling and folding procedure once more and let stand for 1 hour more.

Prepare the desired filling.

Roll the dough out about ½ cm. thick. Place spoonfuls of desired filling on one side. Fold the edge over, pressing lightly. With the edge of a plate, cut out crescent shaped pastries. Place them in a wet oven pan. Brush them with egg yolk. Bake in the oven for 25-30 minutes until they are golden brown.

## TALAŞ İÇİ
### MEAT FILLING FOR PASTRIES

| |
|---|
| 900 gr. mutton (without fat) |
| 5 large onions |
| 2 tablespoons margarine |
| 1 large tomato or 1 tablespoon tomato paste |
| 2 teaspoons thyme |
| 1 bunch of parsley |
| 1 teaspoon salt |
| 1 teaspoon pepper |

Chop one of the onions.

Cut the meat in small strips of 1 cm. wide, 2-3 cm. long.

Melt the margarine, add the onions and the meat. Cover and cook on medium heat for 15-20 minutes, stirring from time to time, until the juice evaporates. Brown for 10 minutes stirring constantly.

Add salt, peeled and chopped tomato or tomato paste, 1½ glasses of warm water. Cover and let simmer for 1½ hours.

Cut the rest of the onions into lengthwise slices. Add to the meat. Mix well. Cook for ½ an hour more.

Add pepper, oregano and chopped parsley. Mix well and remove from heat.

Ready to be used in flaky pastry (talaş böreği).

## TALAŞ BÖREĞİ
### FLAKY PASTRY WITH MEAT
**6 servings**

| |
|---|
| 350 gr. flour |
| 1½ tablespoons softened margarine |
| 320 gr. margarine |
| ¾ glass water |
| 1 tablespoon salt |
| ½ cup olive oil (to roll the pasties out) |
| 1 egg yolk (over) |
| Meat filling (page 44 ) |

Prepare the dough as described for flaky pastry-I (page 33 ). Leave it for 1 hour.

Prepare the meat filling as described above.

With a rolling pin, roll the dough out to make a rectangular shape of 1 cm. thick. Cut it into 12 equal pieces. Fold the four corners of each square piece and press lightly. Leave for 15 minutes.

Take the pieces of dough, dip them one by one in olive oil and with a rolling pin roll each one out as thin as possible.

Share the meat filling out in the middle of each dough. Fold the four sides over to make small parcels. Place them in a wet oven pan.

Beat one egg yolk with 1 teaspoon of olive oil and 1 tablespoon of water. Brush the pastries with it. Bake them in medium hot oven for 25-30 minutes, until they are golden brown.

*Flaky pastry with meat*

In Turkey, fish of great variety are especially tasty due to the characteristics of the four seas which surround the peninsula of Asia Minor. Particularly the Bosphorus fish are known to be delicious.

The fish are prepared in many different ways: fried, grilled, baked or cooked in olive oil with vegetables.

Among the seafood, the most popular are mussels.

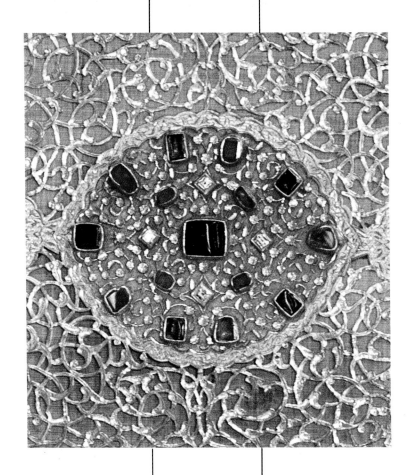

## KILIÇ ŞİŞ
### SWORD FISH ON SKEWERS
**4 servings**

| |
| --- |
| **750 gr. sword fish** |
| **1 tablespoon salt** |
| **1 tablespoon lemon juice** |
| **1 tablespoon olive oil** |
| **1 tablespoon onion juice** |
| **1 teaspoon ground red pepper** |
| **1 dozen bay leaves** |
| **Sauce: Juice of 1 large lemon** |
| **½ cup olive oil** |
| **½ bunch of parsley** |

Put into a bowl the sword fish cut into match-box size pieces. Add salt, pepper, lemon juice, olive oil, onion juice and bay leaves. Mix well and leave in a cool place for 5-6 hours.

Skewer the pieces of fish lengthwise, leaving 1-2 cm. between each piece. Grill them on barbecue fire for 5-6 minutes each side, brushing from time to time with the marinade sauce.

Serve with olive oil mixed with lemon juice and finely chopped parsley, and steamed fresh potatoes.

## BALIK BUĞULAMASI
### STEAMED FISH
**4 servings**

| |
| --- |
| **(With small fish such as red mullets, sardines, anchovies)** |
| **1 kg. fish** |
| **1 cup olive oil** |
| **½ glass water** |
| **1 lemon (sliced)** |
| **Chopped dill and parsley** |
| **Salt** |

*Sword fish on skewers*

Clean the fish and wash them. Place them side by side in a flat pan.

Add the rest of the ingredients. Cover and cook on medium heat for 6-7 minutes.

Let cool before serving.

## KALKAN TAVA
### FRIED TURBOT
#### 4 servings

| |
|---|
| **2 kg. turbot (male)** |
| **1 cup flour** |
| **Salt, pepper** |
| **Lemon** |
| **Oil for frying** |

Wash and drain the turbot, cut into thick slices.

Leave them for 2 hours in a marinade of lemon juice with salt and pepper.

Pat each piece of fish dry with a paper towel and coat with flour.

Fry two or three pieces at a time in the heated olive oil.

Decorate with slices of lemon.

## BALIK KÖFTESI
### FISH FINGERS
#### 6 servings

| |
|---|
| **2 medium size bonitos** |
| **2 medium size onions** |
| **2 slices of dry bread (without crust)** |
| **4 eggs** |
| **½ bunch of parsley** |
| **1½ teaspoons salt** |
| **½ teaspoon pepper** |
| **½ teaspoon cummin** |

*Fried turbot*

| |
|---|
| **½ tablespoon pine nuts** |
| **½ tablespoon currants** |
| **½ glass flour** |
| **1 glass bread crumbs** |
| **1 glass oil** |

Clean and wash the fish. Cook in salted water with 1 peeled whole onion. Remove the bones and shred.

Add the bread (soaked in water and squeezed), 2 eggs, chopped parsley, salt, pepper, cummin, pine nuts and currants. Mix well and knead.

Take large walnut size pieces of it and roll each one in the palms of your hands to shape into fingers.

Dip first in flour, then in 2 beaten eggs and finally in bread crumbs. Fry in heated oil until they are golden brown on all sides. Drain well and serve.

## ISTAKOZ
### LOBSTER

| 1 lobster (of about 30 to 35 cm.) |
| --- |
| 1 carrot |
| 1 onion |
| 2 gloves of garlic |
| 1 tablespoonful of vinegar |
| Salt |
| Parsley |

Scrape the carrot, peel the onion and the garlic. Put them in a large saucepan half-way filled with water, add salt, vinegar and parsley, and bring to boil.

When it starts to boil drop a full lobster in and boil it for about 23 to 27 minutes, depending on the size of the lobster.

Take it out and let cool. Cut the shell with pliers and remove the white meat. Arrange on a serving dish.

Serve with mayonnaise mixed with mustard, vinegar, chopped capers and pickled cucumbers.

## KARİDES ŞİŞ
### PRAWNS ON SKEWERS
**4 servings**

| 24 prawns |
| --- |
| 2 tomatoes |
| 2 bell peppers |
| 1½ lemons |
| 4 bay leaves cut in halves |
| 1 tablespoon oil |
| Salt |

Remove the shells, heads and tails of raw prawns. Clean the backbones if necessary. Wash and drain them. Wet with ½ lemon juice and sprinkle with salt.

Cut the tomatoes and seeded peppers into 4-5 pieces each. Cut the lemon in slices.

*Lobster*

Put alternately prawns, tomatoes, peppers, bay leaves and lemon slices on 4 skewers. Brush with oil. Grill on fire or in the oven for 10 minutes.

Serve with steamed potatoes or rice.

## RAKI SOSLU LEVREK
### SEA-BASS WITH RAKI
### (ANIS SCHNAPS) SAUCE

| |
|---|
| 600 gm filleted sea bass (8 pieces) |
| 1 small onion |
| 20 gm butter |
| 2 tblsp white wine |
| ¼ tsp salt |
| 1 large tomato |
| 1 bunch dill |
| 1 tblsp cream |
| 1 tsp rakı |

Chop the onion and sauté for 5 minutes in the butter.

Add the diced and peeled tomato and the white wine and arrange the slices of sea bass in the pan (a wide shallow pan is necessary).

Add ¼ teaspoon of salt and cook over a low heat for 8 minutes. Arrange the fish in a serving dish.

Mix the raki, cream and chopped dill, add to the gravy in which the sea bass was cooked and boil all together for 3 minutes. Pour this sauce over the fish and serve.

## KARİDES GÜVEÇ
### SHRIMPS CASSEROLE
#### 6 servings

| |
|---|
| 1 kg. small shrimps |
| 3 small tomatoes |
| 3 small bell peppers |
| 1 small onion |
| 120 gr. grated cheese |
| 1 clove of garlic |
| 2 tablespoons oil |
| ½ teaspoon salt |
| ½ teaspoon pepper |

Remove the shells, heads and tails of raw shrimps. Wash and drain them. Sprinkle with salt.

Heat the oil. Lightly brown chopped onion and crushed garlic. Take them out and add to the shrimps.

Cut the peeled tomatoes and seeded bell peppers into small pieces. Add to the sprimps together with some black pepper.

Share them out in 6 small individual casseroles. Cover with roughly grated cheese.

Bake in hot oven for 15-20 minutes.

*Shrimps casserole*

*Fried red mullets*

## BARBUNYA TAVA
### FRIED RED MULLETS
**4 servings**

| |
|---|
| 1 kg. red mullets |
| 1 cup of flour |
| 1 cup of oil for frying |
| 1 lemon |
| Salt, pepper |
| Parsley |

Gut and wash the fish well and leave to drain.

20 minutes before frying, sprinkle them with salt and pepper to taste.

Coat in the flour.

Fry them until golden brown and drain on kitchen paper.

Decorate with sliced lemon and sprigs of parsley.

## FISTIKLI VEYA CEVİZLİ TARATOR
### PINE NUTS OR WALNUTS PASTE

| |
|---|
| 100 gr. pine nuts or walnuts |
| 2 slices of dry bread (without crust) |
| 2 cloves of garlic |
| ½ glass olive oil |
| ¼ lemon juice or vinegar |
| ½ teaspoon salt |

Pound the pine nuts or walnuts in a mortar.

Soak the bread in water. Squeeze by hand to extract excess water. Crumble and add to the nuts, together with crushed garlic and salt.

Slowly add the olive oil and lemon juice or vinegar, beating constantly, to make a smooth paste.

## MİDYE TAVA
### FRIED MUSSELS
#### 4 servings

| |
|---|
| **30 large mussels (without shells)** |
| **150 gr. flour** |
| **10 gr. yeast** |
| **2 tablespoons margarine** |
| **2 eggs** |
| **2 teaspoons salt** |
| **1 glass oil** |
| **Garnish: Pine nuts or walnuts paste, called "tarator"** |
| **(see the previous recipe).** |

Clean the mussels, removing the hairy edges. Wash and drain well. Place them on a dry napkin.

Leave the yeast in ½ cup lukewarm water for 10 minutes.

In a bowl, put 125 gr. flour. Make a hollow in the middle. Put the yeast, melted margarine, 2 egg yolks and 2 tablespoons of lukewarm water. Mix well to make a soft paste. Leave it in a warm place for 1 hour.

Beat the egg whites stiff with a pinch of salt. Add it to the paste and mix well.

Heat the oil in a frying pan. Take the mussels, one by one, dip first in some flour, then into the paste. Drop into the hot oil and fry until golden brown (not more than 3-4 at a time).

Take them out draining well with a skimmer. Serve at once accompanied with pine nuts or walnuts paste.

*Fried mussels*

## MİDYE PİLÂKİSİ
### MUSSELS WITH VEGETABLES
**6 servings**

| |
|---|
| **50 large mussels (without shells)** |
| **2 medium size onions** |
| **2 medium size carrots** |
| **2 medium size fresh potatoes** |
| **1 small celery root** |
| **1 celery stem** |
| **1 large tomato** |
| **5-6 cloves of garlic** |
| **2 teaspoons salt** |
| **2 teaspoons sugar** |
| **½ glass olive oil** |
| **1 bunch of parsley** |

Clean the mussels, removing the hairy edges. Wash them well.

Heat the olive oil. Add onions cut into lengthwise slices and brown them lightly. Add scraped and sliced carrots, peeled and diced potatoes and celery root, chopped celery stem, whole cloves of garlic, peeled and chopped tomato, salt, sugar and 1 glass of water. Cover and cook on medium heat for 15 minutes.

Add the mussels and keep cooking for 10-15 minutes more, until the vegetables are tender.

Let cool. Decorate with chopped parsley before serving.

## BALIK PİLÂKİSİ
### FISH IN OLIVE OIL
### WITH VEGETABLES
**4 servings**

| |
|---|
| **(With fish such as sea-bass, bonito, grey mullet)** |
| **1 kg. fish** |
| **1 carrot** |
| **3 fresh potatoes** |
| **1 small celery root** |
| **2 medium size onions** |
| **5 cloves of garlic** |
| **1 lemon** |
| **2 medium size tomatoes** |
| **Chopped parsley** |
| **2 teaspoons salt** |
| **2 teaspoons sugar** |
| **½ glass olive oil** |

Cut the onions lengthwise in thin slices, brown them lightly in half of the olive oil.

Add potatoes and celery cut in medium size pieces, carrots in slices, garlic, 1½ teaspoons of salt and 3 cups of water. Cover and cook on medium heat for 20 minutes.

Add the fish, cleaned, washed and cut crosswise into thick slices. Add ½ teaspoon of salt and the rest of the olive oil. Cover and cook for 15 minutes more.

Turn the heat off. Add lemon juice and chopped parsley. Let cool before serving.

## USKUMRU DOLMASI
### STUFFED MACKERELS
#### 6 servings

| |
|---|
| 1½ kg. large mackerels |
| 1 glass olive oil |
| 6 large onions |
| 75 gr. walnuts |
| 25 gr. pine nuts |
| 25 gr. currants |
| 1 bunch of dill |
| 1 bunch of parsley |
| ½ teaspoon cinnamon |
| ½ teaspoon allspice |
| ½ teaspoon pepper |
| 1 teaspoon salt |
| For frying: 150 gr. flour |
| 250 gr. fine bread crumbs |
| 4 eggs |
| 1¼ glasses oil |

Clean the mackerels and wash them well. Pressing and stroking with the thumb and index finger, from the tail towards the head, slacken the flesh. Break the fish-bone at 1 cm. above the tail and below the head. Remove the fish-bone, holding it from the upper part and pulling carefully to the left and right. Hold the fish from the tail and stroking it with the other hand, take the flesh out from the head opening. Chop the flesh with a knife. Repeat the same with all the fish.

Heat the olive oil in a saucepan. Add finely chopped onions and brown them. Add crushed walnuts, pine nuts, currants, spices and the flesh of the fish. Sauté for 5 minutes. Add chopped dill and parsley. Mix well and turn the heat off.

Stuff the mackerels tightly with this mixture. Dip them first in flour, then in beaten eggs and finally in bread crumbs.

Heat the oil in a frying pan. Fry the mackerels, 3-4 at a time, until they are golden brown on both sides. Drain well. Let cool before serving.

## MİDYE DOLMASI
### STUFFED MUSSELS
**6 servings**

| 20 large mussels (with shells) |
| --- |
| 5 tablespoons salt |
| Filling: 1 glass rice |
| 5-6 onions |
| ¾ glass olive oil |
| 1 tomato |
| 1 tablespoon pine nuts |
| 1 tablespoon currants |
| 1½ teaspoons salt |

| 3 teaspoons sugar |
| --- |
| 1 teaspoon cinnamon |
| 1 teaspoon allspice |

Prepare the rice filling with the above-listed ingredients as described for rice filling on page 74 . (Dill and mint are not used for this recipe.)

Sprinkle the mussels with salt and let stand for 1 hour.

Clean the shells scraping with a knife and wash them well.

Insert a knife for 2 cm. through the large edge and carefully open them up only on this edge, leaving the other edge united. Remove the hairy parts and wash them.

Stuff the shells with the rice filling and close them. Arrange them first side by side, then in layers in a large saucepan.

Add ¾ glass of water. Place a small plate over the shells. Cover and cook at high temperature for 30 minutes, until the whole water is absorbed.

Let cool before serving with lemon slices.

*Stuffed mussels*

## LÜFER IZGARA
### GRILLED BLUE-FISH
**4 servings**

| |
|---|
| **4 medium size blue-fish** |
| **½ small cup of olive oil** |
| **1 lemon** |
| **Salt** |
| **1 onion** |
| **Parsley** |

Clean, wash and drain the fish. Sprinkle with salt and let stand for an hour.

Lightly brush them with oil, put them on the grill about 5-6 cm. over the fire. Grill for about 8 to 18 minutes depending on the size of the fish.

Arrange them in a dish. Pour over lemon juice mixed with some olive oil. Serve together with onion cut up in slices (cut the onion in slices, rub them with some salt, wash and drain, mix them with chopped parsley).

*Grilled blue-fish*

## HÜNKÂR BEĞENDİ
### EGG-PLANTS PASTE
### WITH MEAT OR CHICKEN
(Sultan's Delight)

| |
|---|
| **1 kg. mutton** |
| **2 tablespoons margarine** |
| **3 medium size onions** |
| **2 medium size tomatoes or 40 gr.** |
| **tomato paste** |
| **2 teaspoons salt** |
| **½ teaspoons pepper** |
| **Egg-plants paste:** |
| **1½ kg. large egg-plants** |
| **2 tablespoons margarine** |
| **2 tablespoons flour** |
| **1½ glasses milk** |
| **50 gr. grated cheese** |
| **2 teaspoons salt** |

Chop the onions and brown them lightly in melted margarine. Add the meat cut into small pieces. Cook them on medium heat for 10 minutes, stirring from time to time.

Peel and chop the tomatoes. Add to the meat. Cook until the juice evaporates. Add salt, pepper and 2 glasses of warm water. Cover and cook on low heat for 1½ hours until the meat is tender.

Egg-plant paste:

Melt the margarine in a saucepan. Add the flour and brown it lightly on medium heat. Leave it aside.

Grill whole egg-plants on gas flame (or wood fire) until they are burnt outside and very soft inside. Hold each egg-plant by the stem and hold it 2-3 seconds under running tap water. Then peel the skin off with a knife. Put it on a carving wood and mash it with a fork. Add it to the flour. Repeat the same with all the egg-plants.

Put the saucepan on medium heat and cook the egg-plants for 5-6 minutes, stirring constantly.

Slowly add warm milk, salt and finally the grated cheese.

Serve immediately together with the meat. (It may also be served with chicken stew.)

## KIYMALI MERCİMEK
### LENTILS WITH MINCED MEAT
**4 servings**

| |
|---|
| **400 gr. lentils** |
| **4 tablespoons margarine** |
| **2 large onions** |
| **200 gr. minced meat** |
| **2 large tomatoes or 2 tablespoons** |
| **tomato paste** |
| **8 glasses meat stock or water** |
| **2 teaspoons salt** |
| **½ teaspoon pepper** |

Soak the lentils in water for a couple of hours.

Melt the margarine in a saucepan. Add finely chopped onions and lightly brown them. Add the meat, salt and pepper. Cook for 15-20 minutes, stirring occasionally, until the juice evaporates. Add peeled and chopped tomatoes or tomato paste and meat stock or water. Cover and let simmer.

Drain the lentils. Put them in 2 litres of boiling water. Cook for 20 minutes. Drain and add to the meat. Cover and cook on low heat for 45-60 minutes, until the lentils are soft.

*Egg-plants stuffed with meat*

## KARNIYARIK

### EGG-PLANTS
### STUFFED WITH MEAT

**6 servings**

| |
|---|
| 6 medium size egg-plants |
| ½ glass oil |
| 3 medium size onions |
| 175 gr. minced meat |
| 2 tablespoons margarine |
| 3 large tomatoes |
| 6 green peppers |
| 1½ teaspoons salt |

Remove the stems of the egg-plants. Peel them leaving lengthwise stripes. On one side, make a deep lenthwise incision with a knife. Leave them in salted water for half an hour.

Chop the onions and brown them in margarine. Add the minced meat and sauté for 10 minutes. Add peeled and chopped tomatoes and salt. Cook until the juice evaporates.

Heat the oil. Drain the egg-plants. Squeeze them by hand to extract excess water and dry them. Fry until lightly brown on all sides.

Place them side by side in a flat pan and split them. Stuff the splits tightly with minced meat. Top each one with a slice of tomato and one whole green pepper. Add a little water. Cover and cook on low heat for 30-40 minutes until the egg-plants are tender.

Serve with rice.

## PATLICAN MUSAKKASI
### EGG-PLANTS MOUSAKA
#### 6 servings

| |
|---|
| 6 medium size egg-plants |
| 1½ tablespoons oil |
| 2½ tablespoons margarine |
| 3 medium size onions |
| 2 large tomatoes |
| 150 gr. minced meat |
| 5 green peppers |
| 1½ glasses meat stock or water |
| 1½ teaspoons salt |

Remove the stems and peel the egg-plants leaving lengthwise stripes. Cut them legthwise in halves and cut these into 3-4 cm. long pieces. Keep them in salted water for half an hour.

Peel and chop the onions. Lightly brown them in margarine. Add minced meat. Sauté them until the juice is evaporated. Add peeled and chopped tomato and salt. Cook until the tomato juice evaporates.

Heat the oil. Take the egg-plants out of the water. Squeeze them by hand to excract excess water. Dry and lightly fry them.

Take them out and arrange in a flat pan. Spread the minced meat over. Cover with slices of tomato and pieces of green peppers. Sprinkle with salt. Cover and cook on low heat for 20-30 minutes.

(You may also bake it in the oven. In this case is should be covered for the first 20 minutes).

Serve with rice.

## KUZU GÜVEÇ
### MEAT CASSEROLE
#### 6 servings

| |
|---|
| 1 kg. mutton, cut into small pieces |
| 1 dozen pearl onions |
| 4 small tomatoes |
| 2 bell peppers |
| 1 clove of garlic |
| 1 tablespoon thyme |
| 2 tablespoons margarine |
| 2 teaspoons salt |
| ½ teaspoon pepper |

Peel the onions. Peel the tomatoes and cut them into four. Seed the bell peppers and cut them into four.

Place all the ingredients in a casserole. Pour melted butter over. Cover and cook on very low heat or in the oven for 2-2½ hours until the meat is tender.

## YAZ TÜRLÜSÜ
### SUMMER VEGETABLE STEW
#### 6 servings

| |
|---|
| 250 gr. mutton |
| 4 tablespoons margarine |
| 2 medium size onions |
| 250 gr. green beans |
| 2 medium size zucchini squash |
| 2 medium size egg-plants |
| 150 gr. okras |
| 3 large tomatoes |
| 6 bell peppers |
| 4 glasses meat stock or water |
| 4 tablespoons vinegar |
| 2 teaspoons salt |

Melt 1 tablespoon of margarine in a saucepan. Add chopped onions and lightly brown them. Add the meat cut into pieces (with bones) and 1 teaspoon of salt. Cover and cook on medium heat for 20-25 minutes, stirring from time to time.

Remove the ends and the strings of the green beans and cut them in halves. Scrape the skin of the zucchinis. Cut them lengthwise into four, then cut each one into 3-4 cm. pieces. Leave the beans and the squash in water.

Peel the egg-plants leaving lengthwise stripes. Cut them lengthwise into four and each one into 3-4 cm. pieces. Leave them in salted water.

Trim the caps of the okras. Sprinkle with salt and vinegar, mix well.

Boil the green beans and the squash in 1 glass of water (or meat stock) with 1 tablespoon of margarine for 15-20 minutes.

Melt 2 tablespoons of margarine in a small saucepan. Drain the egg-plants, squeeze and dry them. Fry them lightly.

Wash the okras. Add them to the green beans and the squash. Spread the meat over the vegetables, together with its sauce. Put a layer of sliced tomatoes, a layer of egg-plants, another layer of sliced tomatoes and bell peppers.

Sprinkle with salt. Add the meat stock or water. Cover and cook on medium heat for 1½ hours.

*Summer vegetable stew*

## PATLICANLI KEBAP
### EGG-PLANTS KEBAB
**6 servings**

| |
|---|
| **1 kg. mutton** |
| **2 tablespoons margarine** |
| **3 tablespoons oil** |
| **2 large onions** |
| **2 medium size tomatoes or** |
| **2 tablespoons tomato paste** |
| **4 medium size egg-plants** |
| **2 teaspoons salt** |
| **½ teaspoon pepper** |

Cut the egg-plants lengthwise into four and each one into 4 cm. long pieces. Leave them in salted water for ½ an hour.

Drain and squeeze them lightly to extract the excess water. Heat the oil and margarine together. Fry the egg-plants lightly. Take them out.

In the same saucepan put half of the meat cut into cubes and sauté them for 2-3 minutes and take them out. Repeat the same for the other half.

In the same saucepan lightly brown the onions cut into thin lengthwise slices. Add peeled and chopped tomatoes or tomato paste. Cook for 2 minutes.

Add the meat, salt, pepper and 2 glasses of warm water. Cover and cook on low heat for 1½ hours until the meat is tender.

Add the fried egg-plants and cook for 30 minutes more.

## PATLICAN OTURTMA
### EGG-PLANTS WITH MINCED MEAT
#### 4 servings

| |
|---|
| 3 large egg-plants |
| ½ glass oil |
| 1½ tablespoons margarine |
| 2 medium size onions |
| 150 gr. minced meat |
| 3 medium size tomatoes |
| 2 small bell peppers |
| ½ bunch of parsley |
| 1 teaspoon salt |
| ¾ teaspoon pepper |

Peel the egg-plants leaving lengthwise stripes and cut them in 2 cm. thick rings. Leave them in salted water for half an hour.

Chop the onions and brown them in margarine. Add and sauté the minced meat for 10 minutes. Add 2 peeled and chopped tomatoes, salt and pepper. Cook until the juice evaporates. Add chopped parsley.

Heat the oil. Drain the egg-plants. Squeeze them lightly to extract excess water. Dry them. Fry until light brown on both sides.

Arrange them side by side in a flat pan. On each one put a heap of minced meat, with a slice of tomato and a ring of bell pepper on top. Pour in from one side 1 glass of water. Cover and cook on medium heat for 30-35 minutes.

Serve with rice.

## STUFFED VEGETABLES (Dolmalar)

Delicious dishes of stuffed vegetables, called ''dolma'', are divided into two groups: those stuffed with minced meat and served warm, usually together with yoghurt; those stuffed with garnished rice cooked with olive oil and served cold as a second course.

## ETLİ DOLMA İÇİ
### MEAT FILLING
### FOR STUFFED
### VEGETABLES-I

| |
|---|
| 500 gr. minced meat |
| 2 tablespoons margarine |
| 2 medium size onions |
| ¾ cup rice |
| 2 medium size tomatoes |
| Dill, salt, pepper |

Chop the onions and brown them lightly in margarine. Add washed rice and ¾ glass of water. Cover and cook on medium heat for 10 minutes, until the water is absorbed.

Remove from heat. Add the minced meat, chopped dill, tomatoes peeled and cut into small pieces, 1 teaspoon salt and ½ teaspoon pepper. Mix them well, kneading for about 5 minutes.

## ETLİ DOLMA İÇİ
### MEAT FILLING
### FOR STUFFED VEGETABLES-II

| |
|---|
| 500 gr. minced meat |
| 2 medium size onions |

| ¾ cup rice |
| --- |
| **Chopped dill** |
| **Salt, pepper** |
| **½ cup water** |

Chop the onions. Add all the other ingredients and mix them well.

This filling is not as tasty as the first one, but it is lighter and easier to prepare.

# ETLİ YAPRAK DOLMASI
## GRAPE LEAVES
## STUFFED WITH MEAT
### 6 servings

| **500 gr. grape leaves in brine** |
| --- |
| **(medium size thin leaves)** |
| **2 tablespoons margarine** |
| **Meat filling (page 64 )** |
| **250 gr. yoghurt** |
| **(if wished, with garlic)** |

Boil some water. Put the leaves in and cook them for about 5 minutes. Drain and let cool.

Remove the stems. If they are too large, divide them in halves and remove the thick middle veins.

Prepare the meat filling (without tomatoes).

Place each leaf on a plate. Put a small walnut size piece of filling on the larger side. Fold the two sides over the filling and roll it on tightly towards the pointed end of the leaf. Arrange them neatly in a saucepan, in tight rows so that they don't open up during the cooking.

Add margarine and 2 glasses of water. Place an upside-down plate on top of them. Cover and cook on low heat for 35 minutes.

Serve warm, together with yoghourt (beaten with some crushed garlic, if wished).

# ETLİ LÂHANA DOLMASI
## CABBAGE LEAVES
## STUFFED WITH MEAT
### 6 servings

| **1 cabbage of 1½ kg.** |
| --- |
| **2 tablespoons margarine** |
| **1 tablespoon tomato paste** |
| **2 tablespoons salt** |
| **Meat filling (page 64 )** |

Prepare the filling.

Cut the cabbage lengthwise into two, remove the hearts. Put them in a large saucepan with 3 glasses of water. Sprinkle with salt. Cover and cook at high temperature for 5 minutes. Turn them over and cook for 5 minutes more. (Leaves should be soft enough to be handled, but not fully cooked, otherwise they will tear apart while being rolled.)

Take them out, drain and let cool. Take the leaves apart, remove the largest veins and cut them in large enough pieces to be rolled like grape leaves.

Place the thick pieces at the bottom of the saucepan.

Place each piece on a plate, put a walnut size piece of filling on one end, fold the two sides over and roll it on like a cigar.

Arrange them side by side in the saucepan, taking care that they don't open up.

Add margarine and tomato paste melted in 2 glasses of water. Place a small lid or plate on top of them. Cover and cook on low heat for 40-45 minutes. Serve warm, with slices of lemon.

## ETLİ KABAK DOLMASI
### ZUCCHINI SQUASH STUFFED WITH MEAT
#### 6 servings

| |
|---|
| 1 kg. medium size zucchini squash |
| 1 tablespoon margarine |
| 3 large tomatoes or |
| 50 gr. tomato paste |
| Dill, salt |
| Meat filling (page 64 ) |

Choose short and rather thick zucchinis. Peel them and cut the ends off. If they are too large, cut them in half.

Cut out conical caps from the larger end of each one; hollow them out with a knife, taking care not to pierce them.

Stuff them with the meat filling and close the open ends with the caps. Place them in a flat pan. Add margarine and 1 glass of water. Cover and cook on medium heat for 20 minutes.

Add 1 tablespoon of salt, tomatoes peeled and cut into small pieces (or the tomato paste dissolved in ½ cup of water) and 2 glasses of water. Cover and cook on medium heat for 20 minutes more, until they are tender.

Arrange them in a serving dish and decorate with dill leaves. Serve warm (if wished, with yoghourt to which some garlic may be addded).

## ETLİ DOMATES DOLMASI
### TOMATOES STUFFED WITH MEAT
#### 6 servings

| |
|---|
| 12 medium size firm tomatoes |
| 3 tablespoons margarine |
| ½ tablespoon salt |
| Meat filling (page 64 ) |

Cut the tomatoes around the top and take the lids off. Remove the pulp with the help of a small spoon. (Cut the pulp into small pieces and use them in the meat filling).

Stuff the tomatoes with the meat filling and put the lids on. Arrange them in a saucepan.

*Tomatoes stuffed with meat*

Add 1½ glasses of water, margarine and salt. Cover and cook on medium heat for 30-35 minutes, until they are tender.

Serve warm (if wished, with yoghourt to which some garlic may be added).

## ETLİ BİBER DOLMASI
### BELL PEPPERS
### STUFFED WITH MEAT
**6 servings**

| 12 medium size bell peppers |
| --- |
| 3 tablespoons margarine |

| ½ tablespoon salt |
| --- |
| Meat filling (page 64 ) |

Cut around the stems of the peppers and open the lids up. Remove the seeds and wash them well.

Stuff the peppers with the meat filling and put the lids on. Arrange them side by side in a saucepan, with the caps upwards.

Add 2½ glasses of water, margarine and salt. Cover and cook on medium heat for 40-60 minutes, until they are tender.

Serve warm (if wished, with yoghourt to which some garlic may be added).

## ETLİ BAMYA
### OKRA WITH MEAT
**4 servings**

| |
|---|
| 750 gr. okra |
| 6 tablespoons margarine |
| 2 large onions |
| 2 large tomatoes |
| 200 gr. mutton |
| 3 green peppers |
| 1 small lemon |
| Salt |
| ½ cup vinegar |

Trim the caps of the okra conically. Wash and drain them. Add 3 tablespoons of salt and the vinegar. Mix them well and leave for half an hour.

Chop the onions and brown them lightly in margarine. Add the meat cut in small pieces and brown for 5 minutes. Add 1 teaspoon of salt, half a cup of water; cover and cook on medium heat for 20 minutes.

Cut the tomatoes into slices, place them over the meat. Wash the okras well and place half of them side by side on top of the tomato slices. Repeat the same with two more layers of tomatoes and okras. Place pieces of green peppers on top of them, add lemon juice, 1 teaspoon of salt and 2½ glasses of water. Cover and cook on medium heat for 50-60 minutes.

## KIŞ TÜRLÜSÜ
### WINTER VEGETABLE STEW
**6 servings**

| |
|---|
| 250 gr. mutton |
| 4 tablespoons margarine |
| 2 medium size onions |
| 3 medium size potatoes |
| 2 medium size celery roots |
| 2 medium size carrots |
| 2 leeks |
| 4 glasses meat stock or water |
| 2 teaspoons salt |

Cook the meat as described for summer vegetable stew (page 60).

Peel the celery roots and cut them into 1 cm. thick slices. Put them in 1 glass of water. Peel the leeks and cut them into 3 cm. long pieces. Add to the celeries

*Okra with meat*

with 1 tablespoon of margarine. Cook on high heat for 15-20 minutes, stirring occasionally. Add them to the meat.

Melt 2 tablespoons of margarine in a small saucepan. Add sliced carrots and potatoes cut into ½ cm. thick slices. Sauté them for 10 minutes. Add them to the meat.

Sprinkle with salt. Pour in the meat stock or water. Cover and let simmer until they are tender.

## TERBİYELİ KEREVİZ
### CELERY ROOTS IN EGG SAUCE
**6 servings**

| |
|---|
| 4 medium size celery roots |
| 4 tablespoons margarine |
| 250 gr. mutton |
| 2 medium size onions |
| 2 teaspoons salt |
| ½ teaspons pepper |
| 3 glasses of meat stock or water |
| 1 egg |
| Juice of 1 lemon |

Melt the margarine in a saucepan. Add chopped onions, meat cut into small cubes, salt and pepper. Cover and cook on medium heat, stirring from time to time, for 2) minutes. (Onions and meat should not be browned, otherwise the celery will change colour.)

Peel the celery roots. Cut them first into halves, then into 1 cm. thick slices and immediately put them into water with the juice of ½ lemon.

Drain the celeries. Cook them for 10 minutes at high temperature, in ½ glass of water or meat stock and 2 tablespoons of margarine.

Put the meat in the center of a flat pan. Arrange the celeries neatly all around. Sprinkle with salt. Pour in rest of the meat stock. Cover and cook on medium heat for 20-30 minutes, until the celeries are tender.

Drain the sauce and keep it warm. Take the meat and celeries upside down onto a serving dish.

In a small bowl, beat the egg with lemon juice. Little by little add from the hot sauce, beating vigorously, until it thickens. Pour it over the meat and celeries. Serve at once.

# ETLİ KURU FASULYE
## WHITE BEANS WITH MEAT

**4 servings**

| |
|---|
| 2 glasses white beans |
| 250 gr. mutton, cut into small pieces |
| 4 tablespoons margarine |
| 2 large onions |
| 2 large tomatoes or 3 tablespoons tomato paste |
| 4-5 glasses meat stock or water |
| 1 green or red pepper |
| Salt |

Soak the beans in cold water for 8-10 hours. Drain. Put them in boiling water and cook on medium heat for 30 minutes, until they are half done. Drain them.

Chop the onions and brown them lightly in margarine. Add the meat and cook them, stirring from time to time, until the juice evaporates.

Add peeled and chopped tomatoes or the tomato paste, the pepper cut into 4-5 pieces and 2 teaspoons of salt. Cover and cook on very low heat for 45 minutes.

Add the beans and the stock. Cover and let simmer until the beans are tender.

Sprinkle with red pepper before serving with rice and mixed pickles.

## ETLİ NOHUT
### CHICK-PEAS WITH MEAT
**4 servings**

| |
|---|
| **2 glasses dreid chick-peas** |
| **250 gr. mutton, cut into small pieces** |
| **4 tablespoons margarine** |
| **2 large onions** |
| **2 large tomatoes or** |
| **2 tablespoons tomato paste** |
| **4-5 glasses meat stock or water** |
| **1 green or red pepper** |
| **Salt** |

Proceed the same way as described for white beans with meat (page 70;). The only difference is that the chick-peas should be soaked in "salted" water.

## LÂHANA FIRIN
### CABBAGE AU GRATIN
**6 servings**

| |
|---|
| **1 cabbage of 1½ kg.** |
| **250 gr. minced meat** |
| **2 large onions** |
| **6 tablespoons margarine** |
| **2 glasses meat stock or water** |
| **50 fr. grated cheese** |
| **2 tablespoons tomato paste** |
| **1 flass milk** |
| **3 eggs** |
| **2 teaspoons salt** |
| **½ teaspoons pepper** |

Remove the outer leaves and hard parts of the cabbage. Chop, wash and drain.

Melt the margarine in a saucepan. Add finely chopped onions and brown them. Add the minced meat and sauté them until the juice evaporate.

Add chopped cabbage, salt and pepper. Cook at high tempera stirring from time to time, for 30-35 minutes.

Add the tomato paste dissolved in 2 glasses of meat stock of water. Cover and cook on low heat until the cabbage is soft and the whole stock evaporates. Let cool.

Arrange the cabbage in a flat oven pan. Sprinkle with grated cheese. Beat the eggs in a bowl. Mix with milk. Pour over the cabbage.

Bake in the oven for 30-40 minutes.

Cut into square portions before serving.

Different kinds of fresh vegetables take a great part in Turkish cookery. Usually vegetables are not eaten as simple garnishings with meat, but prepared as tasty dishes on their own. Apart from the warm vegetable dishes with or without meat, an important and tasty part of the Turkish food is "vegetables cooked with abundant olive oil", garnished with salt, sugar, onions and sometimes garlic, and served cold, usually as a second course.

The most notable among these vegetables is the egg-plant which can be prepared in so many different ways, starting with egg-plant salad and going up to stuffed egg-plants; there is even a dessert and a marmelade prepared with egg-plants!

## İMAM BAYILDI
### EGG-PLANTS IN OLIVE OIL
### (IMAM'S DELIGHT)
**6 servings**

| |
|---|
| 6 medium size egg-plants |
| 6 medium size onions |
| 3 large tomatoes |
| 8 cloves of garlic |
| 1½ teaspoons salt |
| 4 teaspoons sugar |
| 1 glass olive oil |
| ½ bunch of parsley |

Cut the onions in thin lengthwise slices. Brown them in olive oil, together with peeled cloves of garlic.

Add peeled and chopped tomatoes.

Remove the stems of the egg-plants. Peel them in lengthwise stripes. Cut them lengthwise into halves.

Place the egg-plants side by side in a flat pan. Spread the onion and tomato mixture over them. Sprinkle with salt and sugar.

Pour in 2 glasses of water. Cover and cook on medium heat until they are very soft.

Let cool. Arrange the egg-plants on a serving dish. Heap the onions and tomatoes on each one. Decorate with chopped parsley. Carefully pour the sauce in from one side.

## ZEYTİNYAĞLI KEREVİZ
### CELERY ROOTS IN OLIVE OIL
**6 servings**

| |
|---|
| 3 medium size celery roots |
| 2 large onions |
| 6 small carrots |
| 3 medium size fresh potatoes |
| ½ glass olive oil |
| 2 teaspoons salt |
| 4 teaspoons sugar |
| 1 lemon |
| ½ bunch of parsley |

Peel the celery roots and cut them into 2 cm. thick rings. Put them immediately in water with the juice of one lemon.

*Egg-plants in olive oil*

Heat the olive oil in a saucepan. Add coarsely chopped onions and brown them lightly. Add scraped carrots and peeled potatoes cut into small cubes. Sauté them for 5 minutes.

Add the celery rings, salt, pepper and 1½ glasses of water with lemon juice. Cover and cook on low heat for 45 minutes until the celeries are tender.

Let cool. Arrange the celery rings on a serving dish. Heap onions, potatoes and carrots on each ring. Pour the sauce over. Top each one with chopped parsley.

## ZEYTİNYAĞLI DOLMA İÇİ
### RICE FILLING FOR STUFFED VEGETABLES

| |
| --- |
| **1 glass rice** |
| **6-7 medium onions** |
| **¾ glass olive oil** |
| **1 medium size tomato** |
| **25 gr. pine nuts** |
| **25 gr. currants** |
| **½ bunch mint or 1 tablespoon dried mint** |
| **1 bunch dill** |
| **½ teaspoon pepper** |
| **2 teaspoons salt** |
| **4 teaspoons sugar** |
| **1 teaspoon cinnamon** |
| **1 teaspoon allspice** |

Cover the rice with lukewarm water and let cool. Pour the water out, wash well and drain.

Chop the onions finely. Add the nuts, 1 teaspoon salt and the olive oil. Brown them on medium heat, stirring constantly, for about 20 minutes.

Add the drained rice and toast them for 10 minutes. Add peeled tomato cut into small pieces, rest of the salt, pepper, sugar, and ¾ glass of warm water. Mix them well and cover the lid. Turn the heat down as soon as it starts boiling. Let simmer for 10-15 minutes, until the water is absorbed.

Add the spices and chopped herbs. Cover well with a cloth underneath the lid leave in its own steam for half an hour. Mix well with a wooden spoon before using for recipes.

## ZEYTİNYAĞLI YAPRAK DOLMASI
### GRAPE LEAVES STUFFED WITH RICE
**6 servings**

| |
|---|
| **250 gr. grape leaves** |
| **(large and thin ones)** |
| **½ lemon** |
| **Rice filling (see page 74 )** |

Prepare the rice filling.

Put the leaves in boiling water and cook for 5 minutes. Drain and remove the stems. Place the stems at the bottom of the saucepan. (If the leaves are too large, remove the middle veins and divide each into two.)

Place each leaf on a plate. Put ½ tablespoon of filling on the larger end of it, fold the two sides over and roll it on like a cigarette.

Place them tightly side by side in a saucepan. Add lemon juice and 1 glass of water. Put a small lid or plate on top of them. Cover and cook on low heat for one hour, until the sater is absorbed.

Let cool. Arrange on a serving dish and serve with lemon slices.

*Grape leaves
stuffed with rice*

## ZEYTİNYAĞLI LÂHANA DOLMASI
### CABBAGE LEAVE STUFFED WITH RICE
**6 servings**

| |
| --- |
| 1 cabbage of 1½-2 kg. |
| 1 tablespoon olive oil |
| 1 tablespoons lemon juice |
| 3 tablespoons salt |
| Rice filling (without dill and mint) |
| (page 74 ) |

Cut the cabbage lengthwise into two, remove the hearts. Put them in a saucepan with 5 cups of water. Sprinkle with salt. Cover and cook at high temperature for 5 minutes. Turn them over and cook for another 5 minutes until they are tender enough to be stuffed and rolled, but not fully cooked, otherwise they will tear apart.

Take them out of the water, drain and let cool. Take the leaves apart, remove the large veins and cut them into hand size pieces. Place the thick pieces at the bottom of the saucepan.

*Artichokes in olive oil*

Place each piece on a plate. Put one tablespoonful of rice filling on the larger end. Fold the two sides over the filling and roll it on like a cigar.

Place them neatly side by side in the saucepan. Add lemon juice, olive oil and 1 glass of water. Sprinkle with some salt. Cover and cook on low heat for 45-60 minutes, until the whole water is absorbed and the leaves sare tender.

Serve cold with lemon slices.

## ZEYTİNYAĞLI PATLICAN DOLMASI
### EGG-PLANTS STUFFED WITH RICE
**6 servings**

| |
|---|
| **6 large egg-plants** |
| **¾ glass olive oil** |
| **1 teaspoon salt** |
| **Rice filling (page 74 )** |

Remove the stems of the egg-plants. Cut out conical caps from this end. Hollow them out with a sharp knife. Wash them add leave in salted water.

Rub the pulp with some salt and squeeze them in order to take the juice out. Cook the pulp together with the rice filling.

Stuff the egg-plants with the filling and close the ends with the caps. Place them side by side in a saucepan. Sprinkle with salt. Add 1 glass of water. Cover and cook on low heat for 45-60 minutes, until they are tender.

Let them cool before serving.

## ZEYTİNYAĞLI BİBER DOLMASI
### BELL PEPPERS STUFFED WITH RICE
**8 servings**

| |
|---|
| **16 medium size bell peppers** |
| **4 small tomatoes (optional)** |
| **¼ glass olive oil** |
| **1 teaspoon salt** |
| **Rice filling (page 74 )** |

Cut around the stems of the peppers. Remove the seeds. Wash and drain them.

Stuff the peppers, not very tightly, with the rice filling and close them either with their own lids or with caps cut out from tomatoes. Place them side by side in a saucepan, with the lids upwards.

Sprinkle with salt and olive oil. Add ¾ glass of water. Cover and cook on low heat for 45-60 minutes, until the whole water is absorbed and the peppers are tender.

Let them cool before serving.

## ZEYTİNYAĞLI YEŞİL FASULYE
### GREEN BEANS IN OLIVE OIL
#### 6 servings

| |
|---|
| 1 kg. green beans |
| 1 glass olive oil |
| 3 medium size onions, chopped |
| 2 large tomatoes |
| 1 green pepper |
| 2 teaspoons salt |
| 3 teaspoons sugar |

Remove the two ends and the strings of the beans, trimming the two sides. Cut them in half. Wash and drain.

Heat the olive oil. Lightly brown the chopped onions and the green pepper cut in 3-4 pieces. Add the tomatoes peeled and cut into small pieces. Add the beans, salt and sugar. Mix well. Pour in warm water just enough to cover them.

Cover and cook on low heat for 1 hour until the beans are tender and the sauce is reduced.

Let cool before serving.

## ZEYTİNYAĞLI ENGİNAR
### ARTICHOKES IN OLIVE OIL
**8 servings**

| |
|---|
| 8 large artichokes |
| 18 pearl onions |
| 3 medium size fresh potatoes |
| 1 medium size celery root |
| 3 small carrots |
| Juice of 1½ lemon |
| 2 tablespoons flour |
| 1 glass olive oil |
| 1 tablespoon salt |
| 2 tablespoons sugar |

In a large saucepan put 10 glasses of water, 2 tablespoons of flour and the juice of 1 lemon. Mix well.

Add peeled onions, peeled tomatoes, celery root and carrots, all of them cut into small cubes.

Remove the leaves of the artichokes and trim them well leaving only the fleshy middle part. Leave only 2-3 cm. of the stems. Put each one immediately into the water with the other vegetables.

Take the artichokes out of the water and arrange them side by side in a large pan. Add the other vegetables, olive oil, sugar, salt, ½ lemon juice and 5 glasses of the same water in which the vegetables used to be.

Cover and cook on medium heat for 1 hour, until the artichokes are well tender.

Let cool before serving.

*Zucchini squash croquettes*

## YOĞURTLU KABAK KIZARTMASI
### FRIED ZUCCHINI SQUASH WITH YOGHOURT
**6 servings**

| |
|---|
| 1½ kg. zucchini squash |
| 300 gr. flour |

| 1 glass oil |
| --- |
| 500 gr. yoghourt |
| 2-3 cloves of garlic |
| 2 teaspoons salt |

Peel the zucchinis, remove the stems and cut them lengthwise into thin slices (3-4 mm.). Sprinkle with salt and let stand for 1 hour.

Put the flour in a flat bowl. Stirring constantly, pour in 1½ glasses of water to make a soft and smooth paste.

Heat the oil. Dry the zucchini slices, dip them in the flour paste and fry them golden brown (not more than 4-5 at a time).

Serve with yoghourt beaten with crusted garlic and some salt.

## ZEYTİNYAĞLI PIRASA
### LEEKS IN OLIVE OIL
#### 6 servings

| 1 kg. leeks |
| --- |
| 1 medium size carrot |
| ½ glass olive oil |
| 2 tablespoons rice |
| 2 teaspoons salt |
| 4 teaspoons sugar |
| ½ bunch of parsley |
| 1 lemon |

Clean the leeks, remove the green ends and cut them into 3-4 cm. long pieces. Wash and drain.

Scrape the carrot and cut it into slices.

Heat the olive oil. Add the leeks and carrots. Cook on medium heat for 15-20 minutes, stirring from time to time.

Add washed rice, salt, sugar and 2 glasses of water. Mix well. Cover and cook on low heat for 40 minutes, until the leeks are tender.

Let cool. Put in a serving dish. Decorate with chopped parslay. Serve with slices of lemon.

## BARBUNYA PİLÂKİSİ
### FRESH CRANBERRY BEANS IN OLIVE OIL
#### 6 servings

| 1 kg. fresh cranberry beans |
| --- |
| 2 bell peppers |
| 2 medium size onions |
| 2 medium size tomatoes |
| 1 medium size carrot |
| 4-5 cloves of garlic |
| ¾ glass olive oil |
| 2 teaspoons salt |
| 3 teaspoons sugar |
| ½ bunch of parsley |
| 1 lemon |

Sheel the beans. Put them in boiling salted water and cook on medium heat for 15 minutes. Drain them.

Heat the olive oil in a saucepan. Add chopped onions and brown them lightly. Add bell peppers, seeded and cut into pieces, together with scraped and sliced carrot. Stir for 1-2 minutes. Add tomatoes peeled and cut into small pieces and whole cloves of garlic. Finally add the beans, salt and sugar. Mix well.

Pour in enough water to cover them. Cover the sauceplan and cook on medium heat until the beans are tender.

Let cool. Decorate with coarsely chopped parsley. Serve with lemon slices.

## KABAK MÜCVERİ
### ZUCCHINI SQUASH CROQUETTES
**6 servings**

| |
|---|
| 3 medium size zucchini squash |
| 2 medium size onions |
| 100 gr. mashed white cheese |
| (optional) |
| 1 small tomato |
| 1 bunch of dill |
| ½ bunch of parsley |
| 1 teaspoon salt |
| ½ teaspoon pepper |
| 1 teaspoon dry mint |
| 4 eggs |
| 3 tablespoons flour |
| 1½ glasses oil |

Peel the squash. Wash and grate them. Sprinkle with salt. Knead and squeeze by hand to extract excess juice. Drain well.

Add grated onions, cheese, peeled and chopped tomato, chopped dill and parsley, salt, pepper, mint, eggs and flour. Mix well.

Heat the oil in a frying pan. Put in tablespoonful amounts of the mixture (4-5 at a time) and fry both sides. Serve at once.

*Steamed lamb with vegetables*

The large variety of meat dishes include grilled meats, roasts, stews, casseroles and the famous "köftes", i.e. different kinds of meatballs.

One important kind of meat is the "döner kebab" which you only get in restaurants or in big banquets. This is made of layers of lamb meat on a big vertical skewer which slowly turns in front of a vertical grill. While the meat is slowly done, thin pieces of it are vertically cut with a special long knife and served with garnished rice.

## TERBİYELİ KÖFTE
### "KÖFTE" IN EGG SAUCE
**6 servings**

| |
|---|
| 750 gr. minced mutton or beef |
| 1 large onion |
| 2 tablespoons rice |
| 1 tablespoon margarine |
| 1 bunch of parsley |
| 2 teaspoons salt |
| ½ teaspoon pepper |
| Sauce: 2 egg yolks or 1 whole egg |
| Juice of 1 lemon |

Wash the rice and boil for 15 minutes in 2 glasses of water. Drain. Add it to the minced meat, together with grated onion, salt and pepper. Knead for 5 minutes.

In the palms of your hands, roll small walnut size balls and put them in a tray containing finely chopped parsley. Shake the tray so that the parsley sticks onto the meat balls.

Boil 2½ glasses of salted water with margarine. Drop the meatballs into it. Cover and cook on medium heat for 20 minutes.

In a small bowl beat 2 egg yolks or 1 whole egg with lemon juice. Beating vigorously, slowly add ½ glass of the boiling meat stock. Add it to the saucepan. Turn the heat off. Mix well and serve.

## KUZU BUĞULAMASI
### STEAMED LAMB WITH VEGETABLES
**4 servings**

| |
|---|
| 1 kg. of lamb (leg cut in large pieces) |
| 50 gr. margarine |
| 2 medium size carrots |
| 6 fresh potatoes |
| 2 onions |
| 2 laurel leaves |
| 2 teaspoons thyme |
| Salt, pepper |

*Steamed lamb with wegetable.*

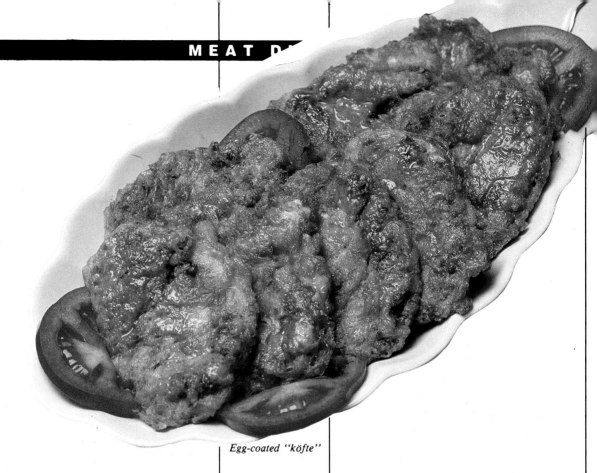

*Egg-coated "köfte"*

## KADINBUDU KÖFTE
### EGG-COATED "KÖFTE"

("woman's thigh")

**6 servings**

| |
| --- |
| **750 gr. minced meat (not very greasy)** |
| **2 large onions** |
| **½ cup rice** |
| **1½ tablespoons margarine** |
| **4 eggs** |
| **2 teaspoons salt** |
| **½ teaspoon pepper** |
| **1 glass oil** |

Heat the margarine in a saucepan. Lightly brown chopped onions. Add rice, some salt and 1 glass of water.

Lightly brown in margarine pieces of meat together with the onions, peeled and cut in slices. Add salt and pepper. Pour over enough water to cover them and cook over medium heat during 40 minutes.

Scrape the carrots and cut them in slices; peel the potatoes and cut them in medium size pieces. Add them to the meat. Let simmer on low heat during half an hour.

Arrange them in a dish, sprinkle with thyme before serving.

Cover and cook on medium heat until the rice is soft and the water is absorbed. Let cool.

Put half of the meat in a saucepan and sauté it at high temperature until the juice evaporates. Add it to the other half and mix well.

Add 2 eggs, salt, pepper and the rice with onions. Knead for 5 minutes.

Take egg size pieces of this mixture and roll each one in the palms of your hands to give flat and oval shapes.

Heat the oil. Beat 2 eggs in a bowl. Dip each ''köfte'' in beaten eggs and fry on medium heat, until they are golden brown on both sides.

Serve at once, with steamed potatoes.

## İSLİM KEBABI
### STEAM KEBAB
**6 servings**

| |
|---|
| **1 kg. mutton (with bones)** |
| **4 tablespoons margarine** |
| **3 large onions** |
| **3 medium size tomatoes** |
| **3 medium size egg-plants** |
| **3 medium size bell peppers** |
| **2 teaspoons salt** |
| **½ teaspoon pepper** |

Place the meat cut into pieces of 150 gr. at the bottom of a saucepan. Put layers of peeled onions cut into four, peeled and chopped tomatoes (2 of them), egg-plants cut first lengthwise then into 3-4 cm. pieces, seeded bell peppers cut into 2-3 pieces, one tomato cut into slices, margarine, salt, pepper and ½ glass of water. Cover very tightly to keep the steam inside and cook on very low heat for 1½ - 2 hours.

## ÇÖMLEK KEBABI
### MEAT AND VEGETABLE CASSEROLE
**6 servings**

| |
|---|
| **1 kg. mutton** |
| **4 tablespoons margarine** |
| **1 dozen pearl onions** |
| **150 gr. green beans** |
| **1 large egg-plant** |
| **2 medium size fresh potatoes** |
| **2 medium size carrots** |
| **2 large tomatoes** |
| **50 gr. okras** |
| **2 bell peppers** |
| **2 teaspoons salt** |
| **½ teaspoon pepper** |
| **½ bunch of dill** |

In a large earthenware casserole, place the meat cut into cubes. Then arrange in layers: 1/3 of tomatoes cut into slices, green beans cut in halves, scraped carrots cut into short sticks, egg-plant cut lengtwhise into four and then into pieces, peeled onions, 1/3 of tomatoes in slices, seeded bell peppers cut into four, peeled potatoes cut into large cubes, okras without caps and the rest of the tomatoes cut into slices.

Sprinkle with salt, pepper and chopped dill. Add margarine and ½ glass of water. Cover and cook on very low heat for 2 hours until the meat is tender.

## SIĞIR PAPAZ YAHNİSİ
### BEEF RAGOUT
**6 servings**

| |
|---|
| **800 gr. lean beef** |
| **4 tablespoons margarine** |
| **500 gr. pearl onions** |
| **10 cloves of garlic** |
| **3 tablespoons vinegar** |
| **1 teaspoon cinnamon** |
| **1 teaspoon allspice** |
| **2 teaspoons salt** |
| **½ teaspoon pepper** |

Melt the margarine in a saucepan. Add the meat cut into large dice and cook on medium heat until the juice is evaporated.

Add peeled whole cloves of garlic and onions. Brown for 4-5 minutes.

Add vinegar, spices and 4 glasses of warm water. Cover and cook on low heat for 3 hours, until the meat is tender.

Serve with rice.

## BEYKOZ USÛLÜ PAÇA
### TROTTERS
(the Beykoz way)
**6 servings**

| |
|---|
| **12 large trotters** |
| **12 glasses of water** |
| **10-12 cloves of garlic** |
| **1 tablespoon olive oil** |
| **½ tablespoon salt** |
| **12 slices of bread** |
| **4 tablespoons oil** |
| **Sauce: 1 tablespoon flour** |
| **1½ tablespoons margarine** |
| **5 egg yolks** |
| **Juice of 2 lemons** |
| **1 teaspoon salt** |

Put the cleaned trotters in a large saucepan, together with peeled whole cloves of garlic, olive oil and salt. Cover with water. Cook on low heat (removing the scum when it starts boiling) for 8-10 hours until they are tender. Take them out. Remove the bones without breaking the meat into pieces. Keep the sauce warm.

Heat the oil in a frying pan. Fry slices of bread on both sides. Arrange them side by side in a flat dish. Place trotters meat on each slice of bread.

Melt the margarine in a small saucepan. Add the egg yolks, salt, lemon juice and flour, mixing well. Beating constantly and keeping it on very low heat, slowly add from the trotters sauce. Pour this sauce over the meat. Warm it ip for 2-3 minutes. Serve at once. (You may pour over 2 tablespoons of heated butter mixed with ground red pepper.)

## YOĞURTLU KEBAP
### KEBAB WITH YOGHOURT
**4 servings**

| |
|---|
| **750 gr. mutton, cut into cubes** |
| **(or 500 gr. minced meat,** |
| **made into meat balls)** |
| **6 slices of bread** |
| **500 gr. yoghourt** |
| **3 tomatoes** |
| **4 hot green peppers** |
| **3 tablespoons butter** |
| **Salt, black and red pepper** |
| **Parsley** |

Leave the meat cubes in a marinade of sliced onions, olive oil, salt and pepper.

Peel and chop the tomatoes. Cook with 1 tablespoon of butter. Keep warm. (Tomatoes may be replaced by 2 tablespoons of tomato paste, dissolved in 1 cup of water.)

Cut toasted slices of bread into cubes. Arrange them on a serving dish. (In Turkey, the bread may be replaced by "pide", a special kind of flat bread.)

Grill the meat (or meatballs made with 1 small grated onion, 1 slice of dry bread soaked in water and crumbled, salt and pepper). Grill also the green peppers. Arrange them on pieces of bread.

Pour first beaten yoghourt, then tomato sauce, finally melted hot butter. Sprinkle with ground red pepper. Decorate with parsley leaves. Serve at once.

## KİMYONLU SAHAN KÖFTESİ
### CUMMINS "KÖFTE"
**6 servings**

| |
|---|
| **750 gr. minced meat** |
| **2 small onions** |
| **3 slices of dry bread (without crust)** |
| **3 large tomatoes or 2 tablespoons** |
| **tomato paste** |
| **2 cloves of garlic** |
| **2 teaspoons salt** |
| **½ teaspoon pepper** |
| **2 teaspoons cummin** |
| **1 glass oil** |

Soak the bread slices in water. Squeeze by hand to extract excess water. Crumble and add to the minced meat, together with grated onions, crushed garlic, salt, pepper and cummin. Knead well for 10 minutes.

Take large walnut size pieces of this mixture and roll each one in the palms of your hands into round and flat shapes.

Heat the oil in a pan. Lightly brown the meatballs on both sides. Take them out and arrange in a flat pan. Spread on them peeled and chopped tomatoes or the tomato paste dissolved in a glass of water. Sprinkle with salt. Cover and cook on medium heat for 20-25 minutes.

(Instead of chopped tomatoes, you can put slices of potatoes, tomatoes and bell peppers on each meatball.)

*Cummins "köfte"*

## TAVUK KÖFTESİ
### CHICKEN CROQUETTES
**6 servings**

| |
|---|
| 300 gr. chicken meat |
| 2 tablespoons margarine |
| 3 tablespoons flour |
| ¾ glass milk |
| 1 cup grated cheese |
| 3 egg yolks |
| 1 teaspoon salt |
| ½ teaspoon pepper |
| For frying: ½ glass flour |
| 2 eggs |
| 1 glass bread crumbs |
| 1 glass oil |

Melt the margarine in a saucepan. Add the flour and brown for two minutes. Slowly add the milk, stirring constantly. Add grated cheese, egg yolks, salt and pepper and cook for 5 minutes stirring all the time. Turn the heat off.

Add cooked chicken meat torn into small pieces. Mix well and leave in the refrigerator for 2-3 hours.

Take large walnut size pieces of the mixture and roll each one in the palms of your hands to shape them into fingers.

Dip them first in flour, then in beaten eggs, finally in bread crumbs.

Heat the oil in a frying pan. Fry them until golden brown. Drain well. Serve at once.

## TAVUK YAHNİSİ
### CHICKEN STEW
**8 servings**

| |
|---|
| 2 chickens |
| 4 tablespoons margarine |
| 2 large onions |
| 2 cloves of garlic |
| 3 large tomatoes or 2 tablespoons tomato paste |
| 2 teaspoons salt |
| ½ teaspoon pepper |

Divide the chickens into large pieces. Sauté them in margarine on high heat for 8 minutes.

Add salt, garlic and onions cut into lengthwise slices and brown them.

Add peeled and chopped tomatoes or tomato paste dissolved in ½ glass of water and black pepper. Cover and cook on low heat for 1½ hours until the chickens are tender.

Serve with rice or steamed potatoes, or egg-plant purée.

## PİLAVLI TAVUK KIZARTMASI
### ROAST CHICKEN WITH PILAFF
**4 servings**

| |
|---|
| 1 whole chicken |
| 500 gr. rice |
| 1 tablespoon margarine |
| 1 onion |
| 1 carrot |

| |
|---|
| **2 medium size tomatoes** |
| **100 gr. green peas (canned)** |
| **Salt, pepper** |
| **Oil** |

*Roast chicken with pilaff*

Cover the rice with hot salted water and let it stand until it gets cool.

Clean and wash the chicken. Put it in a casserole together with peeled onion, scraped carrot, salt and pepper. Cook over medium heat until it gets soft.

Take it out of the stock, tear it up in large pieces and brown them in some oil.

Melt the margarine in a saucepan. Sauté the tomatoes peeled and cup up in small pieces. Add 3 glasses of chicken broth and the rice. Cook over low heat until the liquid is absorbed. Add the peas, cover and let stand for 15 minutes.

` Mix well with a wooden spoon, put it in a large dish. Arrange the chicken pieces on top.

## İÇLİ KÖFTE
### CRUSTED MEATBALLS
**8 servings**

| |
|---|
| 750 gr. minced meat |
| 1½ glasses of fine "bulgur" |
| (boiled and pounded wheat) |
| 1 egg |
| ½ cup crushed walnuts |
| 1 tablespoon pine nuts |
| 1 tablespoon currants |
| 3 onions |
| 1 tablespoon margarine |
| 1 glass oil |
| 1 teaspoon salt |
| 1 teaspoon pepper |
| 1 teaspoon cummin |
| ½ teaspoon ground red pepper |
| 1 bunch of parsley |

Melt the margarine in a saucepan. Brown the finely chopped onions together with the pine nuts. Add half of the minced meat. Sauté and cook until the juice evaporates. Remove from heat.

Add salt, pepper, cummin, crushed walnuts, currants and chopped parsley. Mix well.

In a bowl, mix the "bulgur" with the other half of the meat. Add salt, pepper, red pepper and egg. Knead well, sprinkling with some water now and then.

Take a big walnut size piece of it in the palm of your hand. With the index finger of the other hand, make a hole into it, and press to the sides to make the inside bigger and the walls as thin as possible.

Stuff it with the meat filling and close the hole bringing the sides together.

Squeeze it in wet palms of your hands to shape in into a semi-sphere.

Repeat the same until you finish the meat.

Cook them in simmering salted water for 5 minutes. Drain well with a skimmer.

A just before serving, fry them in hot oil until golden brown on all sides.

## AVCI KEBABI
### HUNTER'S KEBAB
**4 servings**

| |
|---|
| 1 kg. mutton |
| 3 tablespoons margarine |
| 3 medium size onions |
| 2 medium size tomatoes or |
| 50 gr. tomato paste |
| 3 medium size fresh potatoes |
| 3 medium size carrots |
| 50 gr. green peas |
| 2 teaspoons salt |
| ½ teaspoon pepper |

Melt the margarine in a saucepan. Add peeled onions cut into 7-8 pieces, meat cut into pieces and tomatoes cut into four (or the tomato paste). Cook on medium heat for 25-30 minutes, until the juice is absorbed.

Add salt and 2½ glasses of warm water. Cover and cook on low heat for about 1½ hours.

Add peeled potatoes cut into large cubes and scraped carrots cut into thick slices. Cover and cook on low heat for 25 minutes until the vegetables are tender.

## ADANA KEBABI
### PIQUANT KEBAB

| |
|---|
| **1 kg minced beef** |
| **500 gm lamb fat** |
| **2 onions** |
| **2 bunches parsley** |
| **salt and black pepper** |
| **5 large onions** |
| **To garnish:** |
| **5 large onions** |
| **2 bunches parsley** |
| **1 clove garlic** |
| **tomatoes** |
| **green peppers** |

Put the beef and lamb fat through the mincer together. Add 2 bunches onions, salt and pepper, 3 teaspons of salt and 1 teaspoon of black pepper and knead thoroughly.

With meaty hands wipe the special broad-bladed skewers needed for shish meat balls to ensure that the mixture will stick.

Taking an egg-sized piece of the mixture at a time, put it on a skewer and shape it around the skewer, elongating it to a length of about 10 cm.

Grill on both sides.

Cut the onions into thin slices and mix with the crushed garlic and chopped parsley. Garnish each piece of grilled kebab with this mixture.

Serve with grilled tomatoes and green peppers on flat pide bread.

*Piquant kebab.*

*Broiled "köfte"*

## IZGARA KÖFTE
### BROILED "KÖFTE"
**6 servings**

| |
|---|
| **750 gr. minced mutton** |
| **(not very greasy) or minced beef** |
| **(from shoulder) or a mixture of both** |
| **(minced twice)** |
| **4 slices of dry bread (without crust)** |
| **1 large onion** |
| **2 teaspoons salt** |
| **½ teaspoon pepper** |
| **½ teaspoon cummin** |
| **1 teaspoon "köfte" spice** |
| **2 tablespoons olive oil** |

Soak the bread slices in a bowl of water. Take them out and squeeze by hand to extract excess water. Crumble them.

Add grated onion and spices. Mix well.

Add the meat, which should be minced twice. Knead until the mixture is smooth.

Take walnut size pieces and roll each one in the palms of your hands into a ball, then press them into a flat and oval shape.

Brush with olive oil and broil on barbecue fire for 5-6 minutes (or in a non-stick frying pan, brushed with a few drops of oil).

## KURU KÖFTE
### "KÖFTE" FINGERS
**6 servings**

| |
|---|
| 750 gr. minced mutton or beef |
| (minced twice) |
| 2 thick slices of dry bread |
| (without crust) |
| 1 large onion |
| 1 bunch of parsley, chopped |
| 1 whole egg |
| 3 teaspoons salt |
| ½ teaspoon pepper |
| ½ teaspoon cummin |
| 1 teaspoon "köfte" spice |
| 1 glass oil |

Soak the bread in water. Squeeze by hand to extract excess water. Crumble. Add all the other ingredients (except the oil). Knead it well for 10 minutes.

Take egg size pieces of this mixture and roll each one in the palms of your hands to shape them into fingers.

Heat the oil in a frying pan. Fry the meat fingers on medium heat.

Serve them hot, together with fried potatoes. They may also be served cool the next day.

## ORMAN KEBABI
### FOREST KEBAB
**4 servings**

The same as hunter's kebab, except for the tomatoes, which should be replaced by 1 tablespoon of oregano to be added when it is done.

## KUZU İNCİK KEBABI
### LAMB SHANKS KEBAB
**6 servings**

| |
|---|
| 6 lamb shankends (1 kg.) |
| 4 tablespoons margarine |
| 3 medium size onions |
| 2 medium size tomatoes |
| 3 medium size egg-plants |
| 5 medium size bell peppers |
| 100 gr. cream |
| 1 lemon |
| 2 tablespoons salt |
| ½ teaspoons pepper |

Melt the margarine in a saucepan. Add the lamb shanks and one chopped onion. Brown them for 10 minutes. Add 2 glasses of water and the juice of one lemon. Cover and cook on medium heat for 40 minutes.

Arrange the meat in a flat saucepan. Cover with egg-plants cut lengthwise into four and then into 3-4 cm. long pieces, seeded bell peppers cut into lengthwise strips, two onions cut into lengthwise slices, peeled and chopped tomatoes, cream, salt and pepper. Cover and cook on medium heat for 30 minutes more.

## TAS KEBABI
### BRAISED MUTTON
**6 servings**

| |
|---|
| 1 kg. mutton |
| 2 tablespoons margarine |
| 2 medium size onions |
| 2 medium size tomatoes or |
| 2 tablespoons tomato paste |
| 1 teaspoon salt |
| ½ teaspoon pepper |

Heat the margarine. Add the meat cut into cubes and fry them on medium heat. Take them out.

Chop the onions and brown them in the same margarine.

Add peeled and chopped tomatoes or the tomato paste dissolved in ½ cup of water, salt, pepper and the meat. Mix well and add 2 glasses of warm water. Cover and let simmer for 2 hrs. until the meat is very tender.

## DÖNER KEBAP
### TURNING GRILLED MEAT

Although it is not possible to prepare this specialty of grilled meat at home (due to the lack of a special upright broiler), we will explain how the meat is prepared just for interest's sake.

| |
|---|
| 10 kg. of lean lamb (from leg) |
| 100 gr. salt |
| 50 gr. pepper |
| ½ lt. onion juice |
| 1 lemon |
| 1 cup olive oil |
| 1 kg. lamb fat |
| 1 kg. minced lamb meat |
| 1 egg |
| ½ cup milk |

The meat should be boned and the skin removed, cut into large thick slices and pound a little with a mallet.

Prepare a marinade of onion juice, lemon juice, milk, olive oil, salt and pepper. Soak meat in this marinade for 12 hours.

Soak lamb fat in warm water.

Mix the minced lamb with the egg.

Skewer the meat, the lamb fat and the minced meat alternately, using larger pieces at the top.

Put the skewer upright in front of the upright grill. The meat is broiled upright turning slowly all the time.

Cut thin slices of meat with a special, very long and sharp knife. Serve on top of flat bread called "pide" or with rice.

*Turning grilled meat*

## SEBZELİ KÂĞIT KEBABI
### LAMB KEBAB WITH VEGETABLES IN PAPER
**6 servings**

| |
|---|
| 1 kg. lamb meat (without bones) |
| 2 medium size onions |
| 3 tablespoons margarine |
| 2 small tomatoes or |
| 2 tablespoons tomato paste |
| 2 small carrots |
| 100 gr. green peas |
| 2 bunches of dill |
| 1 tablespoon vinegar |
| 2 tablespoons thyme |
| 3 tabléspoons oil |
| 2 teaspoons salt |
| ½ taespoon pepper |
| 2 large sheets of wax-paper |

Melt the margarine in saucepan. Add the meat cut into egg size pieces and brown on all sides.

Add finely chopped onions, scraped carrots cut into small sticks, one bunch of chopped dill and some salt. Cook on medium heat, stirring from time to time, until the juice is absorbed.

Add vinegar and peeled and chopped tomatoes or tomato paste dissolved in very little water. Cook for 5 minutes more.

Add 1 glass of warm water. Cover and cook on medium heat for 1-1½ hours until the meat is tender.

Take the meat and carrots out·with a skimmer. Strain the sauce.

Heat the oil. Lightly fry peeled potatoes cut into small cubes. Take them out and add them to the carrots, together with preserved green peas, chopped dill and oregano.

Cut up 6 pieces of wax-paper (20 × 30 cm.) In the middle of each one, put one piece of meat, 2-3 tablespoons of vegetables and some sauce. Fold the sides over to make a parcel (taking care that the sauce does not leak out).

Place the parcels side by side in an oven dish. Slightly wet them with water. Bake them in hot oven for 15 minutes.

Serve in their parcels.

## SAC KEBABI
### "SAC" KEBAB
**4 servings**

| |
|---|
| 1 kg. mutton |
| 5 large onions |
| 2 tablespoons oil |
| 1 tablespoon margarine |
| 2 medium size tomatoes or |
| 2 tablespoons tomato paste |
| 2 teaspoons salt |
| ½ teaspoon pepper |

Heat the oil and margarine together. Put the meat cut into ½ cm. wide and 2-3 cm. long strips, and brown them stirring constantly.

Peel and cut the onions into thin lengthwise slices. Add half of them to the meat and brown them.

Add peeled and chopped tomatoes or tomato paste dissolved in ½ cup of water. Cook until the juice is absorbed. Add the rest of the onions, salt and pepper. Cook for 5 minutes more.

Add 2 glasses of warm water. Cover and cook on low heat for 1½ hours until the meat is tender.

## Kuzu Düğün Kızartması
### Lamb Wedding Roast
#### 6 servings

| |
|---|
| 1 kg. lamb meat, cut into large pieces |
| 2 large onions |
| 100 gr. margarine |
| ½ kg. small fresh potatoes |
| 2 teaspoons salt |
| ½ teaspoon pepper |
| 1 glass oil |

Melt the margarine in a saucepan. Lightly brown the meat. Add onions cut lengthwise into slices. Brown for 5 minutes. Add salt, pepper and 1 glass of water. Cover and cook on low heat for 1½ hours.

Heat the oil. Peel the potatoes, cut them into walnut size pieces. Fry them in the oil. Take them out when they are half done.

Put the meat in an oven dish. Arrange the potatoes around. Pour the sauce over. Bake in hot oven for 20 minutes.

## Kuzu Kapamasi
### Lamb Stew
#### 4 servings

| |
|---|
| 1 kg. lamb meat (with bones) |
| 3 tablespoons margarine |
| 1 onion |
| 3 green salads |
| 12 green onions |
| 1 bunch of dill |
| 2 teaspoons salt |

The meat should be from loin or shoulder parts of the lamb, cut together with the bones into large onion size pieces. (In Turkey, you should ask your butcher to cut the meat for "kapama".)

In a saucepan put the meat, washed green onions cut into small pieces, whole leaves of green salads, peeled onion cut into 7-8 pieces, salt and 2 glasses of water. Cover and cook on low heat for 1½ hours, until the meat is very tender. Add chopped dill, cook for 3 minutes more and serve.

## ŞİŞ KEBAP
### SHISH KEBAB
**6 servings**

| |
|---|
| 1 kg. mutton (from shoulder or thigh, without fat) |
| 1 tablespoon olive oil |
| 1 medium size onion |
| 2 teaspoons salt |
| 3 small tomatoes (optional) |
| 3 bell peppers (optional) |
| 1 tablespoon oregano (optional) |

Cut the meat into 2-3 cm. dice. Add olive oil, salt and onion juice. (Slice the onion lengthwise. Sprinkle with salt. Let stand for 10 minutes. Rub and squeeze by hand to extract the juice). Leave for 1-2 hours.

Skewer the meat (alternating with pieces of tomatoes and peppers, if wished) leaving ½ cm. between each piece.

Grill on barbecue fire for 2-3 minutes each side.

Sprinkle with salt and oregano.

*Shish kebab*

## KUZU ANKARA TAVA
### ANKARA LAMB ROAST
**6 servings**

| |
|---|
| 1 kg. lamb meat, cut into large pieces |
| 2 tablespoons margarine |
| 2 teaspoons salt |
| 2 onions |
| 1 carrot |
| ½ glass preserved green peas |
| 500 gr. yoghourt |
| 1 tablespoon flour |
| 2 egg yolks |

Melt the margarine in a saucepan. Brown the meat for 7-8 minutes. Add onions cut into lengthwise slices. Brown for 5 minutes more.

Add salt and 4 glasses of water. When it starts boiling, remove the froth with a skimmer. Cover and cook on low heat for 45 minutes. Add sliced carrots. Cook for 30 minutes more.

Drain the sauce and reduce it to 2½ glasses. Arrange the meat, carrots and peas in an oven dish.

In a small saucepan carefully mix the yoghourt with flour. Slowly add the boiling meat sauce, stirring constantly. Beat in 2 egg yolks.

Pour the sauce over the meat. Bake in hot oven for 10-15 minutes, until it is golden brown.

## BAHÇIVAN KEBAP
### GARDENER'S KEBAB
**4 servings**

| |
|---|
| 1 kg. mutton |
| 3 tablespoons margarine |
| 20 pearl onions |
| 150 gr. preserved green peas |
| 1 zucchini squash |
| 150 gr. green beans |
| 2 bell peppers |
| 2 medium size tomatoes |
| 1 bunch of dill |
| 2 teaspoons salt |
| ½ teaspoon pepper |

Melt the margarine in a saucpan. Add the meat cut into cubes and cook them, stirring from time to time, until the juice is absorbed.

Add peeled onions. Cover and cook on low heat, stirring occasionally, for 15 minutes.

Add peeled and chopped tomatoes, green beans cut into halves, bell peppers cut into rings, salt, pepper and 1 glass of water. Cover and cook on low heat for 45 minutes, until the meat is half cooked.

Add scraped squash cut into pieces and green peas. Cook for half an hour more. Add chopped dill and remove from heat.

The rice is an important dish in the Turkish cookery, prepared in many different ways and each one so delicious that it can be served as a dish on its own. The preparation of a rice dish (pilaf) is not a simple procedure of boiling the rice as a garnishing for the meat; it requires a careful procedure of measuring the exact amounts of rice and water and of the cooking time, in order to have a tasty rice dish in separate grains rather than a sticky one. Garnished rice is also used as filling for stuffed vegetableb and grape leaves.

## SADE PİRİNÇ PİLAVI
### PLAIN PILAFF
**4 servings**

| |
|---|
| **2 glasses of rice** |
| **3 tablespoons of butter** |
| **3 glasses of water or stock** |
| **2 teaspoons salt** |
| **½ teaspoon sugar** |

Place the rice in a bowl, cover it with hot salted water. Let stand until it gets cool. Wash thoroughly and drain well.

Melt the butter in a saucepan. Add the water or stock, the rice, salt and sugar. Mix well, cover and let simmer for 15 minutes.

Remove from heat and let stand for another 15 minutes. Mix well with a wooden spoon before serving.

*Plain pilaff*

## SULTAN REŞAT PİLÂVİ
### SULTAN RESHAD RICE
#### 6 servings

| |
|---|
| 2 glasses rice |
| 3 glasses water |
| 6 tablespoons butter |
| 200 gr. minced meat |
| 1½ tablespoons margarine |
| 2 medium size tomatoes or |
| 2 tablespoons tomato paste |
| 1 small onion |
| 1 slide of dry bread (without crust) |
| 2 teaspoons salt |
| ½ teaspoons sugar |
| ½ teaspoons pepper |

Wash the rice. Cover with warm water and let cool. Wash 3-4 times and drain well.

Melt the butter in a saucepan. Add the rice and brown for 10 minute. Add water, salt and sugar. Cover and cook on medium heat until the water evaporates. Let stand on very low heat.

Soak the bread in water. Squeeze the excess water out. Crumble and add to the minced meat, together with grated onion, salt and pepper. Knead for 5 minutes. Roll in the palms of your hands into tiny balls.

Melt the margarine in a saucepan. Lightly brown the meatballs. Add peeled and chopped tomatoes or tomato paste. Cook for 5 minutes. Add 1/3 glass of water. Cook for 15-20 minutes.

Mix the rice with a wooden spoon. Heap it onto a round serving dish. Make a hollow in the middle. Fill it up with the meatballs. Serve at once.

## PATLICANLI İÇ PİLÂV
### GARNISHED RICE WITH EGG-PLANTS
#### 6 servings

| |
|---|
| 2 glasses rice |
| 4 medium size onions |
| 2 medium size tomatoes |
| 1 glass olive oil |
| ½ kg. egg-plants |
| 1 tablespoon pine nuts |
| 1 tablespoon currants |
| 1 teaspoon cinnamon |
| 1 teaspoon allspice |
| 2 teaspoon salt |
| 4 teaspoon sugar |
| ½ teaspoon pepper |
| 1 bunch of dill |

Cover the rice with salted lukewarm water. Leave for 20 minute. Wash 3-4 times and drain.

Peel the egg-plants leaving lengthwise stripes. Cut them legnthwise into four, then each one into 3-4 cm. pieces. Leave them in salted water for 15-20 minutes.

Heat the olive oil in a saucepan. Drain and dry the egg-plant pieces. Lightly brown them in olive oil and take them out.

In the same saucepan, put chopped onions and pine nuts. Brown them on medium heat. Add the rice and brown for 10 minutes, stirring constantly. Add peeled and chopped tomato, salt, pepper, sugar, currants, fried egg-plants and 3 glasses of water. Cover and cook on medium heat for 10 minutes.

Add the spices and chopped dill. Cover well and let simmer on very low heat for 20 minutes.

Let cool. Mix well with a wooden spoon before serving.

## İÇ PİLÂV
### GARNISHED RICE
**6 servings**

| |
|---|
| **2 glasses rice** |
| **3 glasses meat or chicken stock or water** |
| **4 tablespoons margarine** |
| **1 medium size onion** |
| **1 medium size tomato** |
| **¼ sheep liver or 2 chicken livers** |
| **1 tablespoon pine nuts** |
| **2 tablespoon currants** |
| **1 bunch of dill** |
| **2 teaspoons salt** |
| **3 teaspoons sugar** |
| **1 teaspoon cinnamon** |
| **1 teaspoon allspice** |
| **½ teaspoon pepper** |

Cover the rice with salted lukewarm water. Leave for 20 minutes. Wash 3-4 times and drain.

Melt the margarine in a saucepan. Add cleaned and diced liver and sauté lightly. Take them out.

In the same saucepan, put chopped onion and pine nuts. Brown them lightly. Add the rice. Brown on high heat for 10 minutes. Add salt, pepper, sugar, currants, peeled and chopped tomato and meat or chicken stock or water. Mix well.

Cover and cook first on medium heat, later on low heat for 15 minutes, until the water is absorbed.

Add the spices and chopped dill. Cover well and let simmer on very low heat for 20 minutes. Turn the heat off and let stand for 20 minutes more. Mix well with a wooden spoon and serve (with roasted chicken, turkey or lamb).

*Garnished rice*

## BULGUR PİLÂVI
### "BULGUR PILAFF"
**6 servings**

| | |
|---|---|
| 2 glasses "bulgur" (boiled and pounded wheat) | |
| 4 tablespoons margarine | |
| 3 medium size onions | |
| 1 large tomato | |
| 3 glasses meat stock or water | |
| ½ tablespoon salt | |

Chop the onions finely, brown them in margarine.

Add washed and drained "bulgur". Brown them stirring constantly for 15 minutes. Add salt, peeled and chopped tomato and meat stock or water. Mix well. Cover and let boil on medium heat for 10 minutes. Then lower the heat and cook until the stock is absorbed.

Leave on very low heat for 20 minutes. Mix well with a wooden spoon and serve.

## ETLİ BULGUR PİLÂVI
### "BULGUR" WITH MEAT
#### 6 servings

| |
|---|
| 2 glasses "bulgur" (boiled and pounded wheat) |
| 6 tablespoons margarine |
| 3 medium size onions |
| 2 tomatoes or ¾ tablespoon tomato paste |
| 500 gr. mutton, cut into cubes |
| 3 glasses meat stock or water |
| 2 teaspoons salt |
| ½ teaspoons pepper |

Wash and drain the "bulgur".

Chop the onions and brown them lightly in 3 tablespoons of margarine. Add the meat. Cover and cook on medium heat, stirring from time to time, until the juice evaporates.

Add 1 teaspoon salt, pepper, peeled and chopped tomatoes or tomato paste and 2 glasses of warm water. Cover and cook until tender. Uncover and cook stirring from time to time until the juice evaporates again.

Add 3 glasses of meat stock and remove from heat.

Melt 3 tablespoons of margarine in a saucepan. Add the "bulgur" and cook at high temperature for 10 minutes, stirring constantly. Add 1 teaspoon of salt and the meat together with its stock. Mix well. Cover and cook gently until the stock is absorbed.

Leave on very low heat for 20 minutes. Mix well with a wooden spoon and serve.

## DOMATESLİ, NOHUTLU VEYA ŞEHRİYELİ PİLÂV
### RICE WITH TOMATOES
(or chickpeas or vermicelli)
#### 6 servings

| |
|---|
| 2 glasses rice |
| 2 big tomatoes or 2 tablespoons tomato paste |
| 3 glasses meat stock or water |
| 3 tablespoons butter |
| 2 teaspoons salt |
| ½ teaspoon sugar |

Wash the rice. Cover it with warm water. Add 1 tablespoon of salt. Let cool. Wash 3-4 times. Drain well.

Heat the margarine in a saucepan. Add peeled and chopped tomatoes (or the tomato paste dissolved in ½ glass of water). Cook for 1-2 minutes. Add meat stock or water, salt and sugar. When it starts boiling, add the rice and mix well.

Cover and cook first on medium heat, later on low heat until the water is absorbed.

Put a cloth underneath the lid. Let it simmer on very low heat for 15-20 minutes (taking care that it doesn't stick to the bottom).

Let stand for 15 minutes or more. Mix well with a wooden spoon and serve.

(You may replace the tomatoes with cooked chickpeas to be added at the last moment, or vermicelli browned in butter.)

## YALANCI BİBER DOLMASI
### BELL PEPPERS STUFFED
### WITH UNTOASTED RICE
**6 servings**

| |
|---|
| 12 medium size bell peppers |
| ¼ cup olive oil |
| Filling: ¾ glass rice |
| 2 medium size onions, grated |
| 10 fresh green onions, finely chopped |
| ¾ cup olive oil |
| ½ cup water |
| 1 small tomato, peeled and chopped |
| ½ bunch of fresh mints, chopped |
| 1 bunch of dill, chopped |
| ¼ bunch of parsley, chopped |
| 1 tablespoon salt |
| 2 tablespoons sugar |

Cut around the stems of the peppers and open the lids up. Remove the seeds, wash and drain them.

Wash the rice. Add all the other ingredients. Mix well.

Stuff the peppers, not very tightly, with the filling. Close the lids and place them side by side, with the lids upwards,

## MİDYELİ PİLAV
## -ZEYTİNYAĞLI-
### PILAFF RICE WITH MUSSELS
### COOKED IN OLIVE-OIL

| |
|---|
| 500 gm rice |
| 40-50 mussels without shells |
| ½ glass of olive oil |
| 175 gm onion (2 medium size) |
| 1 litre water |
| 4 cups water |
| Salt and black pepper |

Pick over the rice, put it in a pan and cover it with hot water, add 2 tablespoons of salt, and wait till the water gets cold. Place the rice in a sieve and rinse it thoroughly under the tap.

Cut out the bristles from the mussels. Put them in a pan, add half a cup of olive oil, add finely sliced onions, and sauté until the onions are light brown.

Then, add cleaned, chopped tomatoes (or diluted tomato paste) and stir a few times. Add the cleaned mussels, 4 glasses of water, salt and black pepper, and bring it to the boil.

When it boils, add the prepared rice and cook it for 5 minutes on a high heat, then on a medium heat until the water is absorbed. Then, let it simmer on a very low heat for 20 minutes or until the rice gets fluffy.

Serve it hot or cold.

## BUHARA PİLAVI
### BOKHARA PILAFF
**6 servings**

| |
|---|
| 250 gr. lean lamb (cubed) |
| 2 glasses of rice |
| 3 tablespoons butter |
| 50 gr. blanched almones |
| 2 medium sze carrots |
| Salt, pepper |

Cover the rice with salted hot water and let stand until it gets cool. Wash well with cool water and drain.

Cook the meat in 4-5 glasses of water with some salt. (The stock should be reduced to 3 glasses.)

Melt the butter in a saucepan. Lightly brown the blanched almonds. Add the carrots, scraped and cut up in small cubes. Add the rice and sauté them for about 10 minutes. Add the stock. Cover and let simmer until the liquid is absorbed. Remove from heat and let stand for another 15 minutes.

Mix well with a wooden spoon before serving.

## LÂPA
### RICE STEW
#### 4 servings

| |
|---|
| 1 glass of rice |
| 1½ tablespoons margarine |
| 1 medium size onion |
| 1 large tomato |
| 4 glasses meat stock |
| 1 teaspoon salt |

Wash the rice and drain well.

Melt the margarine in a saucepan. Add finely chopped onions and brown them. Add the rice and brown for 5 minutes. Add peeled and chopped tomato, salt and meat stock.

Cover and cook first on medium heat, later on low heat for 20 minutes, until the rice is cooked, but the stock not fully absorbed.

Serve with grilled hot green peppers.

## KARİDESLİ PİRİNÇ PİLAVI
### RICE PILAFF WITH SHRIMPS

| |
|---|
| 500 gm rice |
| 500 gm shrimps |
| 1 litre water |
| 100 gm margarine |
| 1 tbsp vinegar |
| 1 handful of green peas |
| Salt and black pepper |

Pick over the rice, put it in a pan and cover it with hot water. Add 2 table-spoons of salt, and wait till the water gets cold. Place the rice in a sieve and rinse it thoroughly under the tap.

Boil the shrimps in salted water containing 1 tablespoon of vinegar. When cooked, shell the shrimps and put them aside.

Melt the butter in a saucepan, add 1 litre of water or stock, salt and black pepper, and bring to the boil. Toss in the prepared rice and cook on a medium heat until the water is absorbed. Then turn the heat down very low and cook for a further 20 minutes.

Add half of the shelled shrimps to the pilaf and stir them in.

Place the remaining shrimps and the peas into the base of a mould, and fill it up with the pilaf, pressing only lightly. To serve turn the mould upside down onto a dish.

## HAMSİLİ PİLÂV
### RICE WITH ANCHOVIES
**8 servings**

| |
|---|
| **2 kg. fresh anchovies** |
| **2½ glasses rice** |
| **1 large onion** |
| **2 tablespoons pine nuts** |
| **2 tablespoons currants** |
| **2½ tablespoons margarine** |
| **1½ tablespoons dry mint** |
| **1½ tablespoons salt** |
| **1 teaspoon sugar** |
| **½ teaspoon pepper** |

Wash and drain the rice.

Clean the anchovies. Remove the heads, backbones and tails. Wash and drain them. Place half of them neatly in circular raws in a large oiled oven pan (35-40 cm. in diameter) openeng them up with the fleshy parts upwards.

Put the pan in the oven at medium temperature and cook for 25-30 minutes.

Meanwhile heat the margarine in a saucepan. Brown the grated onion together with the pine nuts and salt.

Add the rice and brown them on medium heat for 5-6 minutes more. Add currants, pepper, sugar, mint and 3¾ glasses of warm water. Mix well. Reduce the heat when it starts boiling and cook gently for 8-10 minutes.

Just before the whole water is absorbed, spread the rice over the baked anchovies in the oven. Place the rest of the anchovies neatly over the rice, opened up and the skins facing upwards.

Put them back in the medium oven and bake until the fish are lightly browned, for about ½ an hour.

Serve at once

## ISTANBUL PİLAVI
### ISTANBUL RICE
**6 servings**

| |
|---|
| **2 glasses rice** |
| **2½ glasses chicken broth** |
| **3 tablespoons margarine** |

| | |
|---|---|
| 2 tablespoons almonds (boiled and peeled) | |
| 1 tablespoons pistachio nuts (peeled) | |
| ½ glass green peas | |
| 1 pinch of saffron | |
| 2 chicken livers | |

*Rice with anchovies*

| |
|---|
| 2 teaspoons salt |
| ½ teaspoon sugar |

Wash the rice. Cover with warm water. Let cool. Wash 3-4 times. Drain well.

Melt the margarine. Add the rice and brown for 5 minutes, stirring constantly with a wooden spoon. Add almonds, pistachio nuts and chopped liver. Sauté for 5 minutes more. Add chicken broth, salt, sugar and saffron. Mix well. Cover and cook first on medium heat, then on low heat until the water is absorbed.

Let simmer on very low heat for 10 minutes. Remove from heat and let stand for 20 minutes more.

Mix well with a wooden spoon and serve.

## BEZELYELİ PİRİNÇ PİLAVI
### PILAFF RICE WITH GREEN PEAS

| |
|---|
| 9 dl water |
| 500 gm rice |
| 150 gm shelled peas |
| 60 gm butter |
| salt |

Pick over the rice, place in a bowl and cover it with hot water. Stir in 2 tablespoons of salt and leave to soak until the water cools. Place the rice in a sieve and wash thoroughly under the running tap.

Boil the peas or sauté them in 1 tablespoon of butter until tender.

Melt the butter in a saucepan, add the water and washed rice and salt and boil it rapidly for 5 minutes. Reduce the heat slightly until the water is absorbed. Add the peas then reduce the heat to very low for about 20 minutes until the rice becomes fluffy.

Stir the rice before serving.

Delicious Turkish desserts can be divided in two main parts, apart from the fruit compotes: milk desserts and sweet pastries (with very special names), the latter being quite rich and therefore served with unsweetened clotted cream, especially that of water-buffalo milk, called "kaymak". The sweet pastries go particularly well after a tasty dish of fried or grilled fish. Various sorts of "kadayıf" are made of ready made doughs: the "tel kadayıf" are thin pieces of dried dough that look like threads; the "ekmek kadayıf" is a special kind of loaf; the "yassı kadayıf" are a kind of flat pancakes.

Some of these desserts are served on special occasions, such as wheat pudding (aşure) served on the tenth day of the Moslem month of Muharrem, or saffron-flavoured sweet rice (zerde) served in weddings.

## İNCİR TATLISI
### FIG SWEET

| |
|---|
| ½ kg drieg figs |
| 1 cup ground walnuts and hazelnuts |
| ¼ cup castor sugar |
| ½ cup clotted-cream |

Cut off the stalks of the figs, and with your finger open up the central cavity.

Fill each fig with some of the ground nuts and sugar mixed together, and arrange in a buttered oven tray.

3. Pour 2 cups of water over them and simmer for a few minutes, basting with the juice. Leave to cool.

Serve with cream.

## LOR TATLISI
### GOAT CHEESE PASTRIES

| |
|---|
| 500 gr. goat cheese (lor) |
| 50 gr. butter |
| 50 gr. sugar |
| 20 gr. flour |
| 20 gr. semolina |
| 4 egg yolks |
| ½ teaspoon baking powder |
| Syrup: 3 glasses sugar |
| 2½ glasses water |
| Juice of ½ lemon |

Beat the egg yolks with sugar. Add melted but cool butter, baking powder and mashed goat cheese. Mix well.

Add flour and semolina. Mix well.

Take small lemon sizi pieces of the dough, them ech one in the palms of your hands into a ball. Press and flatten. Place them in an oiled oven pan, leaving 2 cm. in between.

Bake in medium hot oven for 20-25 minutes, until they are golden brown.

Meanwhile boil the syrup and let simmer for 10-15 minutes. Pour it over the pastries. Cover and bake at low temperature for 15 minutes more.

Let cool before serving.

## KÜNEFE
### SHREEDDED WHEAT/CHEESE DESSERT

| |
|---|
| 500 gm shredded tel kadayıf |
| 400 gm dil cheese* |
| 100 gm melted butter |
| For the syrup: |
| 1½ cups sugar |
| 1 cup water |
| 1 tsp lemon juice |

Put the sugar and water in a saucepan and boil for about 15 minutes until it forms a thin syrup. Add the lemon juice and set aside.

Grease a 25 cm cake tin and pour in six tablespoons of the syrup and spread it overt he bottom of the tin.

In a separate bowl mix the tel kadayıf with the melted butter until it is well distributed and arrange half in the greased tin, pressing down well.

Slice the dil cheese and arrange over the kadayıf. Then put the remainder of the kadayıf on top, smoothing and pressing the surface.

Bake at 100°C until the top is golden brown, then turn and cook until the bottom is golden brown.

Remove from the oven and pour the syrup over the top.

Serve hot.

---

* Dil cheese is a mild, saltless yellow cheese which becomes stretchy when melted.

## SÜTLÂÇ
### RICE PUDDING

| |
|---|
| **8 glasses milk** |
| **1½ glasses sugar** |
| **1 cup rice** |
| **¼ cup rice flour** |
| **¼ cup potato starch** |
| **½ teaspoon salt** |
| **Cinamon (optional)** |

Cook the rice in 1½ glasses of water.

Put the milk, salt and rice in a saucepan. Boil and let simmer.

Put the rice flour and potato starch in a bowl. Slowly add ¾ glass of water, stirring constantly, to make a smooth paste. Add it to the boiling milk. Cook for 10 minutes, stirring all the time.

Add the sugar and cook until it thickens, stirring constantly.

Share it out in individual bowls. Let cool. Sprinkle with cinnamon.

## FIRIN SÜTLÂÇ
### RICE PUDDING AU GRATIN

Proceed the same way as described for plain rice pudding in the previous recipe.

Share it out in individual oven-proof bowls. Bake in the oven until there is a brown crust on top.

Let cool before serving.

## SAMSA
### FLAKY PASTRY WITH WALNUTS

| |
|---|
| 2 cups flour |
| 1 tsp salt |
| 1 tsp vinegar |
| 185 gm butter |
| ½ cup water |
| 125 gm hazelnuts |
| 125 gm hazelnuts |
| 25 gm almonds |
| 2½ tblsp semolina |
| ½ cup icing sugar |
| 2 eggs |
| 2 cups water |
| 1 cup water |
| 1 tsp lemon juice |

Sieve the flour, make a dip in the centre and into this place the salt, vinegar and ½ cup water. Knead well, cover with a cloth and set aside for 15 minutes.

Cut the dough into 4 equal pieces. Roll out and in the centre of each place a slice of butter. Fold the sides inwards and set aside for 15 minutes.

Roll out each piece of pastry again, fold into four and set aside for another 15 minutes. Roll out again fold into four and put in the refrigerator for 3 hours.

Mix the semolina, icing sugar, ground walnuts, hazelnuts and almonds in a bowl and mix together. Add 2 eggs and mix into a paste.

Boil 2 cups of sugar with 1 cup water for 15 minutes. Add the lemon juice and leave to cool.

Take the refrigareted dough and roll it out. Fold into three and roll out again to a rectangle 1 cm thick. Cut widthways into slices 10 cm wide.

Form the paste filling into a roll 1 cm in diameter and place lengthways on each slice of pastry. Roll up and squeeze the ends closed. Set aside for 5 minutes.

Bake at 100°C for 30 minutes.

Remove from the oven and pour tha prepared syrup over the top. Serve when cool.

## GÜL REÇELİ
### ROSE PETAL JAM

| |
|---|
| 225 gm fragrant pink rose petals |
| 6¼ cups sugar (1500 gm) |
| 3¾ cups water |
| 9 gm citric asid or |
| 3 tblsp lemon juice |

Place the rose petals and water in a saucepan. Put the lid on and boil until the petals become a palecolour.

Add the sugar and boil with the lid off until the syrup thickens.

Test whether the jam is ready by taking some of the jam on a spoon and dropping it onto a plate. If the last drop keeps its shape, then the jam is ready.

Now add the lemon juice or citric acid dissolved in a little water, bring to the boil once more and then empty the jam into a clean, dry bowl. When it is cold, fill the jam jars and seal.

## TAVUK GÖĞSÜ
### CHICKEN BREAST PUDDING

| |
| --- |
| **7 glasses milk** |
| **1½ glasses sugar** |
| **¾ cup potato starch** |
| **1¼ cups rice flour** |
| **1½ glasses water** |
| **½ teaspoon salt** |
| **½ chicken breast** |
| **Cinnamon** |

Boil a very fresh chicken breast until it is tender.

Cut it crosswise in 5 cm. long pieces. Rub them between the palms of your hands and tear them into very thin fibres.

Wash the fibres 3-4 times in warm water, changing the water each time and squeezing them tightly to extract excess water.

Put the milk, sugar and salt in a saucepan. Melt the sugar and let simmer.

Put the potato starch and rice flour in a bowl. Slowly add from the boiling milk, stirring constantly, to have a smooth paste. Add it to the milk and cook until it starts thickening, stirring all the time.

Take 4-5 spoonfuls of the pudding and add to the chicken fibres. Mix well with a fork and add them to the pudding. Cook on low heat, stirring constantly, until it thickens. (To check the thickness: pour 1 tablespoonful of it in a plate. Let cool and turn it upside down. It should come out without sticking to the plate.)

Pour it out 2 cm. thick in a dry dish. Let cool and cut out in 10 cm. square portions. Roll each one and sprinkle with cinnamon before serving.

*Burnt chicken-breast pudding*

## MUHALLEBİ
### MILK PUDDING

| | |
|---|---|
| **7 glasses milk** | |
| **1¼ glass sugar** | |
| **½ cup potato starch** | |
| **1½ cup rice flour** | |
| **½ teaspoon salt** | |
| **Cinnamon (optional)** | |

Put the milk, sugar and salt in a saucepan. Melt the sugar and let boil, stirring occasionally.

Put the starch and rice flour in a bowl. Slowly add from the boiling milk to make a smooth paste.

Add it to the milk and cook on medium heat, stirring constantly, until it thickens.

Share out in individual bowls. Let cool. Sprinkle with cinnamon.

## KAZANDİBİ
### BURNT CHICKEN BREAST PUDDING

Using the same ingredients as "tavuk göğsü" prepare the pudding as described. Pour it into a 2-3 cm. deep pan. Put it on gas flame and burn the bottom, turning the pan whenever necessary.

Let cool for 3-4 hours. Cut it into 10 cm. square pieces. Take them out with the help of a spatula. Fold them to make thick rolls, with the burnt side upwards.

## KEŞKÜL
### ALMOND CREAM

| | |
|---|---|
| **8 glasses milk** | |
| **1½ glasses sugar** | |
| **1 glass almonds** | |
| **1 glass water** | |
| **1¼ cup rice flour** | |
| **A pinch of salt** | |
| **For decoration:** | |
| **2 tablespoons almonds** | |
| **2 tablespoons pistachio nuts** | |

Boil 1 glass of almonds in 1 glass of water. Peel and grind them twice. Then pound them in a mortar to have an almond paste.

Add 1 glass of warm milk. Mix well and pass it through a sieve.

Add salt to the remaining 7 glasses of milk. Let simmer.

Put the rice flour in a bowl. Slowly add 1 glass of water, stirring constantly, to have a smooth paste. Add it slowly to the boiling milk. Cook on medium heat for 10 minutes, stirring all the time.

Add the sugar and the milk mixed with almonds. Cook until it thickens, stirring constantly.

Share it out in individual bowls. Let cool. Decorate with boiled, peeled and ground almonds and pistachio nuts.

**BAKLAVA**
"BAKLAVA", SWEET FLAKY
PASTRY

| |
|---|
| 250 gr. flour |
| 2 eggs |
| 1 teaspoon salt |
| 1 teaspoon olive oil |
| 200 gr. starch |
| 1 glass melted margarine |
| 1½ glasses ground walnuts or pistachio nuts |
| 3 glasses sugar |
| Juice of ½ lemon |

Sift the flour. Make a hollow in the middle. Put the eggs, salt and 1/5 glass of water. Mix well and knead for 15 minutes. Cover with a damp cloth and leave for half an hour.

Spread the olive oil over the dough. Knead it again for 15 minutes. Cut it into 8 equal pieces and sprinkle each one with starch.

With a rolling pin, roll them out one by one, to make 15 cm. discs; sprinkle each one with starch and put them one on top of the other. Let stand for 15-20 minutes.

Roll them out again, keeping them together, to make a bigger disc. Separate each layer of dough, sprinkle with starch, and roll them out with a thin rolling pin (oklava), to make the sheets as thin as possible (almost transparent). (The layers of dough can be rolled out all together, one on top of the other. But they should be alternated each time, otherwise the outer layers will get bigger while the inner layers will remain smaller.)

Put the doughs one on top of the other and cut them exactly the same size as the baking pan.

Brush the pan with melted margarine. Place 4 layers of dough, brushing each one with margarine. Spread ground walnuts or pistachio nuts. Place the remaining 4 layers of dough, brushing each one with margarine. Cut through the bottom into 4-5 cm. rectangular or triangular pieces. Bake them in medium hot oven for 1 hour, until they are golden brown.

Meanwhile, put the sugar and lemon juice in a saucepan with 2 glasses of water. Boil on medium heat stirring constantly. Let simmer for 15 minutes.

Take the pan out of the oven. Let cool for 10 minutes. Lightly brush with margarine. Pour the syrup over little by little, so that it absorbes the syrup entirely.

Let cool before serving.

## HOŞMERİM
### HOSHMERIM

| |
|---|
| 500 gm cottage cheese |
| 2 tblsp flour |
| 1 cup sugar |

Mash the cheese with a fork and place in a saucepan. Stir over a low heat until it melts.

In another saucepan stir the flour over a low heat until it turns a pale golden colour.

Add the flour and sugar to the cheese and continue to cook, stirring constantly, until drops of fat appear.

Set the pan aside covered for 10 minutes. Eat warm or cold.

## CEVİZLİ ÇÖREK
### WALNUT CAKES

| |
|---|
| 1 kg flour |
| 200 gm melted butter |
| 1 knob fresh yeast |
| 500 gm ground walnuts |
| ½ litre water |
| 1 tblsp warm milk |
| 1 tsp sugar |

Mix the yeast with the warm milk and 1 teaspoon of sugar, add to the flour and melted butter and knead well. Set aside in a warm place for half an hour.

Roll out the pastry into a circle 60 cm in diamater.

Taking egg-shaped pieces of pastry roll them out into circles and place some of the ground walnuts in the centre of each.

Bake in a moderate oven for one hour.

## PORTAKAL PELTESİ
### ORANGE JELLY-PUDDING

| |
|---|
| 3 oranges |
| 1½ glasses of sugar |
| 1½ lt. water |
| 100 gr. potato starch |
| 50 gr. crushed pistachio nuts |

Grate the orange peels into the water and let stand for 1 hour. Remove the orange peels. Add the juice of the oranges and sugar. Let boil.

Dissolve the potato starch in ½ glass of water. Slowly add it to the saucepan and cook for 8-10 minutes, stirring constantly.

Share it out in individual bowls. Let cool. Decorate with crushed pistachio nuts.

## TULUMBA TATLISI
### FLUTED FRITTERS

| |
|---|
| 30 gr. melted margarine |
| 1½ glasses water |
| 230 gr. flour |
| 4 eggs |
| ½ teaspoon salt |
| 1¼ glasses oil |
| Syrup: 1¾ glasses water |
| 2 glasses sugar |
| Juice of ½ lemon |

Boil the syrup and let simmer for 15 minutes.

Melt the margarine in a saucepan. Add water and salt. When it starts to boil, add the flour, mix well and cook on low heat for 6-7 minutes, stirring constantly with a wooden spoon. Let cool.

Add the eggs and knead for 10 minutes. Put the mixture into a forcing bag. Squeeze out 4-5 cm. long knurled pieces into a frying pan with lukewarm oil in it. (Do not fill the pan up completely.)

Put the pan on medium heat and fry them until they are golden brown. Drain well with a skimmer and drop into the cool sprup. Let stand for 15 minutes.

*Fluted fritters*

## REVANİ
### SEMOLINA CAKE

| |
|---|
| 250 gr. fine semolina |
| 50 gr. flour |
| 250 gr. sugar |
| 60 gr. butter |
| 9 eggs |
| Grated lemon peel |
| 100 gr. almonds |
| A pinch of salt |
| For the pan: ½ tablespoon butter |
| 1 tablespoon flour |
| Syrup: 4 glasses sugar |
| 3½ glasses water |
| Juice of ½ lemon |

Butter a high-sided cake pan of 25 cm. in diameter and sprinkle with flour.

Boil the almonds in 1 glass of water. Drain and peel them. Chop with a knife.

Separate the egg yolks and the whites. Beat the whites stiff with a pinch of salt. Beat the yolks with sugar and grated lemon peel for 7-8 minutes until it is creamy.

Add mixed semolina and flour to the egg yolks. Mix well. Add the egg whites and chopped almonds. Mix with a wooden spoon. Add melted but cool butter. Mix well and pour it into the cake pan.

Bake in medium hot oven for 1 hour, until it is golden brown.

Boil the syrup and let simmer for 10 minutes.

Take the pan out of the oven and pour the boiling syrup over. Let cool. Put is upside down in a serving plate. (It tastes better the next day.)

## UN HELVASI
### FLOUR HALVA

| |
|---|
| 250 gr. flour |
| 1 tablespoon pine nuts |
| 125 gr. butter |
| 250 gr. castor sugar |
| 2 glasses water or milk |
| Vanilla |

Melt the butter in a saucepan. Add sifted flour and pine nuts; lightly brown on low heat, stirring constantly for 30-40 minutes.

Add boiling water or milk. Mix well. Cover and leave on very low heat for 20 minutes.

Add the sugar. Cover and let stand for 1 hour. Take tablespoonfuls of it and arrange them in a serving plate.

## VEZİR PARMAĞI
### VIZIER'S FINGERS

Proceed the same way as described for "lady's navel" (page 130), except for the shape of the pastries, which should be rolled like fingers.

## DİLBER DUDAĞI
### BEAUTY'S LIPS

Proceed the same way as described for "lady's navel" (page 130). The only difference is the shape of the pastries: Make large walnut size balls with the dough. Flatten them and fold each one in two to have them look like lips.

## ZERDE
### SAFFRON-FLAVOURED SWEET RICE

| |
|---|
| 125 gr. rice |
| 6 glasses water |
| 1¼ glasses sugar |
| 1 tablespoon arrowroot starch |
| 2 pinches of saffron |
| To decorate with: ½ cup currants |
| ½ cup pine nuts |
| 1 pomegranate |

Wash the rice. Cook in water with sugar for 20-25 minutes.

Leave the saffron in 1 cup of water. Add it to the rice.

Dissolve the arrowroot starch in ½ cup of water. Add it to the rice. Mix well and cook on medium heat for 20-30 minutes, until it thickens.

Share it out in individual bowls. Let cool. Decorate with pine nuts, currants and pomegranate seeds.

## KAYMAKLI KURU KAYISI
### DRIED APRICOTS STUFFED WITH CREAM

| |
|---|
| 250 gr. dried apricots |
| 250 gr. sugar |
| ½ glass water |
| 1 teaspoon lemon juice |
| Clotted cream (kaymak) |

Put the apricots in a saucepan. Add 6 glasses of lukewarm water and leave for 24 hours.

Drain the apricots. Add sugar, water and lemon juice. Cover and cook on medium heat for ½ an hour until the syrup thickens.

Let cool. Into each apricot insert a hazelnut-size piece of clotted cream. Arrange them in a serving dish, with the creamy parts upwards. Pour the syrup over and serve.

## YOĞURT TATLISI
### YOGHOURT CAKE

| |
|---|
| 250 gr. dense yoghourt |
| 350 gr. castor sugar |
| 300 gr. flour |
| 25 gr. butter |
| 3 eggs |
| ½ teaspoon baking powder |
| Syrup: 3 glasses sugar |
| 3½ glasses water |
| Juice of ½ lemon |

Beat the yoghourt with sugar. Add the eggs, melted butter, flour and baking powder. Mix well.

Pour it 3-4 cm. thick into an oiled oven pan. Bake in medium hot oven for 45-50 minutes, until it is golden brown.

Boil the syrup and let simmer for 5 minutes.

Take the pan out of the oven and slowly pour the boiling syrup over. Let cool. Cut into cubes and serve.

## LOKMA
### FRITTER BALLS

| |
|---|
| **200 gr. flour** |
| **200 gr. water** |
| **1 tablespoon butter** |
| **30 gr. yeast** |
| **½ teaspoon salt** |
| **1 glass oil** |
| **Cinnamon** |
| **Syrup: 1¾ glasses sugar** |
| **1½ glasses water** |
| **1 tablespoon lemon juice** |

Boil the syrup and let simmer for 15 minutes. Let cool.

Put the flour in a saucepan. Make a hollow in the middle. Put the yeast, melted butter and salt. Mix a little and slowly add the water. Mix well and make a soft dough. Leave in a warm place for 1 hour.

Heat the oil. Take a handful of dough. Squeeze and let pop out a hazelnut size piece of it between the thumb and the index finger. Cut it off with a wet spoon and drop it into the heated oil.

Repeat the same, wetting the spoon each time, until you have 7-8 of them in the pan. Fry them lightly, stirring occasionally.

Take them out with a skimmer and drain well.

When all of them are lightly browned, fry them a second time until they are golden brown. Drain well and drop into the syrup.

Take them out and serve sprinkled with cinnamon.

## TEL KADAYIF
### THREADS "KADAYIF"

| |
|---|
| **750 gr. "tel kadayıf"** |
| **(ready-made dough in threads)** |
| **350 gr. butter** |
| **2 glasses walnuts or pistachio nuts** |
| **Syrup: 4½ glasses sugar** |
| **3½ glasses water** |
| **Juice of ½ lemon** |

Tease the "tel kadayıf" out. Spread half of it in a high-sided cake pan of 25 cm. in diameter. Spread crushed walnuts

*Fritter balls*

or pistachio nuts over it, and the other half of the "kadayıf". Pour the melted butter over. Bake in medium hot oven for 40 minutes, until it is golden brown.

Boil the syrup and let simmer for 5 minutes.

Take the pan out. Drain excess butter. Slowly pour the boiling syrup over.

Let cool before serving.

# EKMEK KADAYIFI
## BREAD "KADAYIF"

| |
| --- |
| 1 "ekmek kadayıfı" (ready-made bread to make "kadayıf") |
| 6-7 glasses warm water |
| Syrup: 4 glasses sugar |
| 4 glasses water |
| Juice of ½ lemon |
| Clotted cream (kaymak) |

Boil the syrup in a saucepan and let simmer for 20 minutes.

Place the "kadayıf" in a round and flat pan 5-6 cm. larger than the "kadayıf". Add warm water and let stand for 20 minutes, until it swells and softens.

Pressing with a paper napkin, take the excess water off.

-Pour the syrup over the "kadayıf". Put the pan on medium heat and cook for 30-40 minutes, turning the pan whenever necessary, until bubbles of caramel appear on the top.

Remove from heat and leave for 15-20 minutes (do not let cool completely, otherwise it will stick to the bottom), put it upside down into a serving dish.

Let cool. Serve with "kaymak".

# ŞEKERPÂRE
## ALMOND PASTRIES

| |
| --- |
| 500 gr. flour |
| 100 gr. castor sugar |
| 200 gr. butter |
| 1 egg |
| ½ teaspoon baking powder |
| ½ teaspoon salt |
| 15 almonds |
| Syrup: 1½ glasses sugar |
| 1¼ glasses water |
| Juice of ½ lemon |

Boil the syrup and let simmer for 15 minutes. Let cool.

Beat the egg with sugar. Add softened butter and continue beating. Add salt and flour. Knead well.

Take large walnut size pieces from the dough and roll each one in the palms of your hands to make small balls. Press and flatten them slightly. Place them in an oiled oven pan, leaving 2 cm. in between.

With your finger make a hole in the middle of each one, where you put a peeled whole almond.

Bake them in medium hot oven for 35-50 minutes, until they are golden brown.

Pour the syrup over and let stand for 1 hour.

## AŞURE
### WHEAT PUDDING

| | |
|---|---|
| 250 gr. wheat | |
| 50 gr. rice | |
| 50 gr. white beans | |
| 50 gr. fava beans | |
| 50 gr. chick-peas | |
| 100 gr. dried apricots | |
| 100 gr. dried figues | |
| 150 gr. sultanas | |
| 25 gr. pine nuts | |
| 25 gr. currants | |
| 100 gr. walnuts | |
| 100 gr. hazelnuts | |
| 4 lt. water | |
| 1 lt. milk | |
| 3 glasses sugar | |
| 1 pomegranate | |

Soak the wheat, rice, white beans, fava beans and chick-peas separately in water overnight.

Drain them. Cook the rice for 30 minutes in half of the water and blend it into its water.

Boil the wheat in other half of the water. Add the blended rice and cook on low heat for 2-3 hours until the wheat are tender.

Cook the beans and chick-peas separately until they are tender. Remove the skins of the chick-peas.

Add sugar and milk to the wheat. Dissolve the potato starch in 1 glass of water. Add it to the pudding and cook on medium heat, stirring constantly, until it thickens.

*Wheat pudding*

Add cooked white beans, fava beans, chick-peas, sultanas, currants and dried apricots and figues cut into 4-5 pieces. Cook for 10-15 minutes more and share it out in individual bowls.

Let cool and decorate with hazelnuts, walnuts, peeled almonds, pine nuts, currants, sultanas and pomegranate seeds.

## GÜLLAÇ
### RICE WAFERS DESSERT
**4 servings**

This rose-water flavoured dessert is made of extremely thin wafers of rice sold for the purpose, especially during the month of Ramadan.

| |
|---|
| 10 "güllaç" wafers |
| 1½ lt. milk |
| 400 gr. sugar |
| 200 gr. walnuts or blanched almonds (coarsely crushed) |
| 1 tablespoonful rose-water (optional) |
| 50 gr. pistachos (ground) |

Boil the milk. Remove from heat and add the sugar. Mix well until the sugar is dissolved.

Pour the milk into a large circular oven tray and one by one dip the "güllaç" wafers into it. When it softens a little, remove, place on the kitchen board , fold from four edges into the centre. Place a spoonful of walnuts or almonds in the centre and fold like a bundle. Prepare each wafer similarly and arrange them in a serving dish.

Pour over the rest of the milk. Let stand until the milk is completely absorbed. Sprinkle with rose-water. Decorate with some ground pictachos.

## KADIN GÖBEĞİ
### LADY'S NAVEL

| 225 gr. flour |
| --- |
| 85 gr. melted margarine |
| 2 whole eggs |
| 1 egg yolk |
| ½ teaspoon salt |
| 1¼ glasses oil |
| Syrup: 2 glasses water |
| 1¾ glasses sugar |
| 1 tablespoon lemon juice |

Melt the sugar in 2 glasses of water. Add the lemon juice and boil. Let simmer for 15 minutes. Let cool.

Heat the margarine in a saucepan. Add 1½ glasses of water with some salt. Let boil. Add the flour at once and cook on medium heat for 7-8 minutes, stirring all the time with a wooden spoon. Let the dough cool.

Add 2 whole eggs and 1 egg yolk. Mix well and knead for 10 minutes. Oil the palms of your hands. Take large walnut size pieces from the dough; roll each one into a ball, then press lightly to flatten and with your finger make a hole in the middle.

Drop them into a frying pan with lukewarm oil in it. (Do not fill the pan completely, otherwise they will stick together.)

Put the pan on medium heat and fry the doughs until golden brown on both sides. Drain well and drop into the syrup. Leave in syrup for 15 minutes.

Repeat the same with the rest of the doughs, letting the oil cool a little each time.

## AYVA TATLISI
### QUINCES IN SYRUP

| 1 kg. quinces (4 big ones) |
| --- |
| 1½ glasses sugar |
| 2-3 cloves |
| Clotted cream (kaymak) |

Wash and peel the quinces. Cut them into four and remove the cores. Arrange the slices side by side in a flat pan sprinkled with ½ glass of sugar. Put cloves and 2-3 quince seeds. Spread the remaining sugar over them. Cover and

cook on very low heat for 2-2½ hours until they take a dark reddish colour and get slightly caramelized.

Let cool. Arrange them in a serving dish. Pour the syrup over. Put small pieces of clotted cream on each one.

## KABAK TATLISI
### PUMPKIN IN SYRUP

| 1500 gr. pumpkin |
| --- |
| 1¾ glasses sugar |

| 2 glasses water |
| --- |
| 1 glass crushed walnuts |

Seed and peel the pumpkin, and cut it into 2-3 cm. thick slices.

Arrange them in a flat pan. Spread the sugar, pour the water over. Cover and cook on low heat for 50-60 minutes, until they are tender.

Let cool. Arrange them in a serving dish. Pour the syrup over. Sprinkle with crushed walnuts.

*Pumpkin in syrup*

# LOKUM
## TURKISH DELIGHT

"Lokum" is a traditional sweet made of sugar and starch. It is believed that the production goes back to the XVth century and it achieved its final recipe during the XIXth century. Formerly honey and condensed must were used together with flour for its consistency. When the importation of sugar was initiated at the end of the XIXth century, it became the basical ingredient for the "lokum" confection and later the flour was also replaced by wheat starch.

Today the ingredients of "lokum" are certain amounts of sugar, corn starch and water, boiled for a certain time, together with some fruits or nuts or any other flavour. The cooking time differs between 1 to 2 hours, depending on the size of the boiler. The thick substance is then poured into special wooden trays sprinkled with corn starch; it is also sprinkled on top. It stands from 24 to 48 hours until it gets cool and has a flexible consistency. Then the starch is brushed off, it is sprinkled with powdered sugar and cut up into small cubes.

Apart from the plain "lokum", there exists a great variety with fruits such as strawberries, cherries, lemon or orange, with nuts such as pistachios, walnuts or almonds, and other flavours such as mastic, vanilla, coconut, mint, milk cream or rose water. In the provinces, there are many other local types of "lokum".

## İRMİK HELVASI
### SEMOLINA HALVA

| |
|---|
| **500 gr. coarse semolina** |
| **250 gr. butter** |
| **2 tablespoons pine nuts or peeled almonds** |
| **¾ lt. milk** |
| **2 glasses sugar** |
| **Cinnamon** |

Melt the butter in a saucepan. Add the semolina and pine nuts or almonds. Lightly brown on medium heat, stirring constantly with a wooden spoon for 20-25 minutes.

Lower the heat and add the milk. Mix, cover and let simmer on very low heat until the milk is absorbed.

Add sugar. Mix well. Turn the heat off. Cover well and let stand for 1 hour.

Mix well with a wooden spoon. Serve it tepid.

## KURU ÜZÜM HOŞAFI
### SULTANA COMPOTE
**6 servings**

| |
|---|
| **300 gr. sultanas** |
| **250 gr. sugar** |
| **1½ lt. water** |

Wash and pick over the sultanas. Put them in 1½ lt. of water in a saucepan and let them stand for 10-12 hours.

Add the sugar. Cover and cook on medium heat for 5 minutes.

Serve cold.

*Sultana compote*

## KAHVE
### TURKISH COFFEE

Although coffee was first cultivated at the southern edge of the Arab peninsula, it was via Turkey that the fame of coffee spread to Europe. Within just a few years of its introduction into Turkey, hundreds of coffee-houses sprung up in Istanbul alone, and coffee drinking became such an important part of daily and ceremonial life that the sultan's coffee-set was carried during royal processions; every wealthy household had a servant whose sole task was to prepare coffee; and under Moslem law the failure of a husband to provide his wife with coffee was grounds for divorce.

To make Turkish coffee you need the right equipment: a special long-handled pot called "cezve", small coffee cups and a special coffee mill. The coffee beans have to be toasted to the point and ground to a very fine powder.

There are different sizes of "cezve", depending on the number of persons for whom you wish to make coffee, from 1 to 4, because a well-made coffee must have froth on top and you cannot have a good result if you prepare the coffee for 2 persons for example in a pot for 4.

Into your "cezve" you put one cup of water for each person, 1 rounded teaspoon of coffee and 1 rounded teaspoon or less of sugar. The amount of sugar should be known beforehand, i.e. "az şekerli" (with little sugar), "orta" (medium) or "şekerli" (with sugar). Stir well, put over very low heat and bring slowly to boil. As it boils the froth forms on top. Just before it overflows, remove and divide the froth into the cups, bring to boil again and divide the rest out.

# ÇAY
## TEA

A samovar is the best way to make tea, which is one of the most popular beverages in Turkey. Moreover, a samovar is a practical and very elegant addition to the tea table. The water is put in the main body of the samovar, under which there is a small part which contains hot coals to keep the water hot. The small teapot rests on top and the tea, once made, brews in the steam from the simmering water below. Once brewed, the small narrow-waisted tea glasses are filled half-way and then topped up with boiling water from the tap at the lower part of the samovar.

The tea is served in thin glasses in order to show the colour of the tea distinctly. Well-made Turkish tea should be crystal clear and of a deep mahogany-red hue. Indian tea, being stronger in flavour, does not produce such a rich colour without becoming undrinkable.

Turkish tea is grown in the province of Rize on the eastern Black Sea coast, which has a mild climate with high precipitation and fertile soil. The finest tea you can find is served in the cafés of Rize.

The water used for tea-making is almost as important as the tea itself. Chlorinated, hard and other poor quality waters will result in cloudy tea and impair the flavour. The best is fresh spring water.

Althrough electric samovars are available these days, most Turkish households use the practical modern equivalent of a kettle, on which the small teapot rests. Fill the kettle with cold water and put the tea into the teapot (1 teaspoonful for each cup and 1 for the pot). Put the kettle, with the teapot on top, on the heat to boil.

When the water boils, fill the teapot and replace it on top of the kettle, which should still contain plenty of boiling water, and lower the heat to a minimum while the tea brews for about 10 minutes.

A popular addition to tea is the grated rind of the bergamot, a variety of lime grown in Antalya on the Mediterranean coast of Turkey. A small pinch of this added to the dry tea will give a delicious distinctive flavour, like that of Earl Grey.

## AYRAN
### YOGHOURT SHAKE

Refreshing and thirst-quenching in summer, "ayran" is diluted yoghourt shake with salt. It can be purchased ready mixed in bottles or cartons all over Turkey, but the best is home made.

| |
|---|
| ½ kg. natural yoghourt |
| Salt |
| Water |

Whip the yoghourt with a fork or in an electric blender until it is smooth. Add salt and gradually add about 2 cups of water (depending on the consistency of the original yoghourt) and go on whipping until froth develops on top.

## SALEP

If "ayran" is a refreshing drink ideal for hot summer days, salep is equally ideal for winter. It is made of the ground root of certain orchids, known as salep.

| |
|---|
| 50 gr. salep |
| 50 gr. wheat starch |
| 200 gr. sugar |
| 1½ lt. milk |
| 1 cup water |
| Ground cinnamon |

Boil the milk.

In a separate bowl place the sugar, starch and salep. Mix well, gradually add the water, stirring to remove any lumps.

Add to the boiling milk and beat with a whisk as it simmers for about 5 minutes. Remove from the heat when it thickens.

Serve boiling hot in teacups or mugs, sprinkling with ground cinnamon.

## TÜRK ŞARAPLARI
### TURKISH WINES

Some very fine wines are produced in Turkey and top-of-range quality wines are very reasonably priced. All the grape-growing regions have their own local wines, and there are also the wines of such major producers as Kavaklıdere and Doluca, which are available all over Turkey, and include vintage as well as cheaper table wines.

The most famous of Turkey's wine-producing regions are Ankara, Niğde, Nevşehir, Gaziantep, Elazığ, Tokat, Çanakkale, Tekirdağ, İzmir, Manisa and Bozcaada. Some of the famous Turkish white wine grapes are the *Hasan Dede* of Ankara, the *Narince* of Tokat, the *Misket* of İzmir, the *Emin* of Nevşehir and the *Seminyon* of Bozcaada. Famous black grape varieties used for producing red wine are the *Kontra* of Bozcaada, the *Papaz Karası* of Kırklareli, the *Kalecik* of Ankara, the *Sergi Karası* of Gaziantep and the *Öküz Gözü* of Elazığ.

## RAKI

### ANIS DRINK

"Rakı" is a very popular alcoholic drink in Turkey, made of raisin or grape spirit, redistilled with aniseed.

The word "rakı" is believed to derive from "razaki", the variety of grape originally used to make rakı. The alchohol content of rakı is either 45 or 50 degress.

After the liquor has been diluted, it is left to mature for 1 to 3 months in oak casks, before being filtered and bottled.

"Rakı" is served cold in narrow cylindrical glasses. It may be mixed with water or may be accompanied by soda water. It goes particularly well with hors d'oeuvres, among which the simplest and most popular are white cheese and melon. However, it may also be taken as an aperitif.

Spices are largely used in Turkish cooking, mostly to flavour meat and rice dishes. The following are the most important spices and aromatic herbs for the Turkish cookery:

**Dill** (Dereotu): It is indispensable in stuffed vegetable fillings and some fresh vegetable dishes.

**Mint** (Nane): Both fresh and dried, it is also a common ingredient for vegetable dishes and salads.

**Parsley** (Maydanoz): It is the most common ingredient, widely used in meat and vegetable dishes, salads and soups.

**Paprika** (Kırmızı): Is common in a wide range of vegetable and meat dishes.

**Cinnamon (Tarçın):** It is used in rice fillings for stuffed vegetables and also on milk desserts.

**Mixed spices for meat balls** (Köfte baharı): It is a mixture of various spices specially prepared for flavouring meat balls.

**Somac** (Sumak): Is sprinkled on grilled meat or mixed with slices onion as a garnish. Its sour tang pleasantly offers the rich flavour of grilled meat.

**Bay leaves** (Defne): It goes very well with grilled fish.

**Allspice** (Yenibahar): It is indispensable for rice filling and other garnished rice dishes.

**Cloves** (Karanfil): They are often used in jams and compots.

**Red Pepper** (Kırmızı Biber): Is used in many meat and vegetable dishes and soups and pickles. It is most common common in the form of small flakes, known as pul biber.

**Black Pepper** (Kara Biber): Is used in most hot meat and vegetable dishes.

**Thyme** (Kekik): It is sprinkled on grilled meat and used in stews.

**Cummin** (Kimyon): It is used for flavouring some meat dishes and especially the famous "köfte".

**Saffron** (Safran): Is used in Zerde, a dessert.

# PUBLICATION LIST

**TURKEY (BN)** (In English, French, German, Italian, Spanish, Dutch, Japanese ,Turkish)
**ANCIENT CIVILIZATIONS AND RUINS OF TURKEY** (En Anglais)
**ISTANBUL (B)** (In English, French, German, Italian, Spanish, Japonca, Turkish)
**ISTANBUL (ORT)** (In English, French, German, Italian, Spanish, Turkish)
**ISTANBUL (BN)** (İngilizce, Fransızca, Almanca, Italian, Spanish, Japanese, Turkish)
**MAJESTIC ISTANBUL** (En Anglais, German)
**TURKISH CARPETS** (In English, French, German, Italian, Spanish, Japanese)
**TURKISH CARPETS** (En Anglais, German)
**THE TOPKAPI PALACE** (In English, French, German, Italian, Spanish, Japanese, Turkish)
**HAGIA SOPHIA** (In English, French, German, Italian, Spanish)
**THE KARIYE MUSEUM** (In English, French, German, Italian, Spanish)
**ANKARA** (In English, French, German, Italian, Spanish, Turkish)
**CAPPADOCIA** (In English, French, German, Italian, Spanish, Japanese, Turkish)
**CAPPADOCIA (BN)** (In English, French, German, Italian, Spanish, Dutch)
**EPHESUS** (In English, French, German, Italian, Spanish, Japanese, Turkish)
**EPHESUS (BN)** (In English, French, German, Italian, Spanish, Dutch)
**APHRODISIAS** (In English, French, German, Italian, Spanish, Turkish)
**THE TURQUOISE COAST OF TURKEY** (En Anglais)
**PAMUKKALE** (In English, French, German, Italian, Spanish, Dutch, Japanese, Turkish)
**PAMUKKALE (BN)** (In English, French, German, Italian, Spanish, Turkish)
**PERGAMON** (In English, French, German, Italian, Spanish, Japanese)
**LYCIA (AT)** (In English, French, German)
**KARIA (AT)** (In English, French, German)
**ANTALYA (BN)** (In English, French, German, Italian, Dutch, Turkish)
**PERGE** (In English, French, German)
**PHASELIS** (In English, French, German, Turkish)
**ASPENDOS** (In English, French, German)
**ALANYA** (In English, French, German, Turkish)
**The Capital of Urartu: VAN** (In English, French, German)
**TRABZON** (In English, French, German, Turkish)
**TURKISH COOKERY** (In English, French, German, Italian, Spanish, Japanese, Turkish)
**NASREDDİN HODJA** (In English, French, German, Italian, Spanish, Japanese)
**ANADOLU UYGARLIKLARI** (Turkish)

## Maps:

**TURKEY (NET), TURKEY (ESR), TURKEY (West) TURKEY (South West), ISTANBUL, MARMARIS, ANTALYA-ALANYA, ANKARA, İZMİR, CAPPADOCIA**

## NET® BOOKSTORES

**İSTANBUL GALLERİA BOOKSTORE:**
Galleria Ataköy, Sahil Yolu, 34710 Ataköy Tel: (90-212) 559 09 50
**İSTANBUL MERIT ANTIQUE BOOKSTORE:**
Merit Antique Hotel İçi, Laleli  Tel: (90-212) 513 93 00 -513 64 31
**İZMİR BOOKSTORE:**
Cumhuriyet Bulvarı No: 142/B, 35210 Alsancak-İZMİR Tel: (90-232) 421 26 32

# CARPET
*The largest collection of the top quality Turkish Carpets.*